Int
Word for

ALSO AVAILABLE

By both authors:

BP270 A Concise Introduction to Symphony
BP294 A Concise Introduction to Microsoft Works
BP302 A Concise User's Guide to Lotus 1-2-3 Release 3.1
BP306 A Concise Introduction to Ami Pro 3
BP319 Making MS-DOS Work for You
BP336 A Concise User's Guide to Lotus 1-2-3 Release 3.4
BP339 A Concise Introduction to WordPerfect 5.2 for Windows
BP341 MS-DOS 6 Explained
BP343 A Concise Introduction to Microsoft Works for Windows

By Noel Kantaris:

BP232 A Concise Introduction to MS-DOS
BP243 BBC-BASIC86 on PCs. Bk 1 - Language
BP244 BBC-BASIC86 on PCs. Bk 2 - Graphics and Disc Files
BP250 Programming in FORTRAN 77
BP258 Learning to Program in C
BP259 A Concise Introduction to UNIX
BP260 A Concise Introduction to OS/2
BP264 A Concise Advanced User's Guide to MS-DOS
BP274 A Concise Introduction to SuperCalc5
BP279 A Concise Introduction to Excel
BP283 A Concise Introduction to SmartWare II
BP284 Programming in QuickBASIC
BP288 A Concise Introduction to Windows 3.0
BP314 A Concise Introduction to Quattro Pro 3.0
BP318 A Concise User's Guide to MS-DOS 5
BP325 A Concise User's Guide to Windows 3.1
BP330 A Concise User's Guide to Lotus 1-2-3 Release 2.4

A Concise Introduction to Word for Windows

by

N. Kantaris
and
P.R.M. Oliver

BERNARD BABANI (publishing) LTD.
THE GRAMPIANS
SHEPHERDS BUSH ROAD
LONDON W6 7NF
ENGLAND

PLEASE NOTE

Although every care has been taken with the production of this book to ensure that any projects, designs, modifications and/or programs, etc., contained herewith, operate in a correct and safe manner and also that any components specified are normally available in Great Britain, the Publishers and Author(s) do not accept responsibility in any way for the failure (including fault in design) of any project, design, modification or program to work correctly or to cause damage to any equipment that it may be connected to or used in conjunction with, or in respect of any other damage or injury that may be so caused, nor do the Publishers accept responsibility in any way for the failure to obtain specified components.

Notice is also given that if equipment that is still under warranty is modified in any way or used or connected with home-built equipment then that warranty may be void.

First Published - August 1993

British Library Cataloguing in Publication Data:

Kantaris N.
Concise Introduction to WORD for Windows
I. Title II. Oliver, P.R.M.
652.55369

ISBN 0 85934 338 3

Printed and Bound in Great Britain by Cox & Wyman Ltd, Reading

ABOUT THIS BOOK

A Concise Introduction to Word for Windows has been written for those who want to get to grips with the Microsoft Word for Windows word processor and desk top publishing package in the fastest possible time. No previous knowledge is assumed, but the book does not describe how to set up your computer hardware, or how to install Microsoft Windows. If you need to know more about these topics, then may we suggest that you also refer to the book *A Concise User's Guide to Windows 3.1* (BP325), and to either *A Concise User's Guide to MS-DOS 5* (BP318), or *MS-DOS 6 Explained* (BP341), depending on the version of your Disc Operating System. These books are also published by BERNARD BABANI (publishing) Ltd.

This book was written with the busy person in mind. It is not necessary to read several hundred pages covering all there is to know about a subject, when a few selected pages can do the same thing quite adequately! With the help of this book, it is hoped that you will be able to get the most out of Word for Windows and your computer in terms of efficiency, productivity and enjoyment, and that you will be able to do it in the shortest, most effective and informative way.

More emphasis has been placed on an understanding of what we consider to be the critical areas in the program, such as page layout, paragraph styles and the use of frames, than on a general overall description of the package, although we have tried to make the book as complete as possible.

The Word for Windows package is the leading Windows word processor and, we feel, will stand comparison with anything else available today in the marketplace.

If you would like to purchase a floppy disc containing all the files/programs which appear in this, or any other listed book(s) by the same author(s), then fill-in the form at the back of the book and send it to P. R. M. Oliver at the stipulated address.

ABOUT THE AUTHORS

Noel Kantaris graduated in Electrical Engineering at Bristol University and after spending three years in the Electronics Industry in London, took up a Tutorship in Physics at the University of Queensland. Research interests in Ionospheric Physics, led to the degrees of M.E. in Electronics and Ph.D. in Physics. On return to the UK, he took up a Post-Doctoral Research Fellowship in Radio Physics at the University of Leicester, and in 1973 a Senior Lectureship in Engineering at Camborne School of Mines, Cornwall, where since 1978 he has also assumed the responsibility of Head of Computing.

Phil Oliver graduated in Mining Engineering at Camborne School of Mines in 1967 and since then has specialised in most aspects of surface mining technology, with a particular emphasis on computer related techniques. He has worked in Guyana, Canada, several Middle Eastern countries, South Africa and the United Kingdom, on such diverse projects as: the planning and management of bauxite, iron, gold and coal mines; rock excavation contracting in the U.K.; international mining equipment sales and technical back up; international mine consulting for a major mining house in South Africa. In 1988 he took up a Senior Lectureship at Camborne School of Mines in Surface Mining and Management.

ACKNOWLEDGEMENTS

We would like to thank colleagues at the Camborne School of Mines and Exeter University for the helpful tips and suggestions which assisted us in the writing of this book.

TRADEMARKS

Apple LaserWriter and **TrueType** are registered trademarks of Apple Computer, Inc.

HP LaserJet is a registered trademark of Hewlett Packard Corporation.

IBM is a registered trademark of International Business Machines Corporation.

Lotus, 1-2-3 is a registered trademark of Lotus Development Corporation.

Adobe, **ATM** and **Adobe Type Manager** are registered trademarks of Adobe Systems Inc.

Microsoft, Excel, MS-Graph, MS-DOS, MS-Draw, QuickBASIC and **Windows** are registered trademarks of Microsoft Corporation.

dBASE is a registered trademark of Borland International.

WordPerfect is a registered trademark of WordPerfect Corporation.

CONTENTS

1. PACKAGE OVERVIEW

Microsoft's Word for Windows is the best selling Windows word processor and is fully integrated with the Microsoft Windows environment. In all the Windows versions Word has had a leaning towards desk top publishing which offers fully editable WYSIWYG (what you see is what you get) modes that can be viewed in various zoom levels, including full page. Couple this with the ability to include and manipulate full colour graphics and you can see the enormous power of the program. Once you have overcome the first hurdle and started to use Word for Windows, you will find it both intuitive and an easy program to produce the type of word processed output you would not have dreamt possible.

Although Word for Windows is quite happy working with Windows 3.0, the latest versions of the program (version 2.0 and above), have been designed to make full use of the improved features of Windows 3.1. We feel the benefits, which include significant speed improvements and TrueType font support, make it well worth upgrading your environment to Windows 3.1.

Major Features

Some of the major features Word for Windows contains, include the ability to:

- Drag and drop text when editing text and tables in a document - this is more convenient than cutting and pasting.
- Create documents that have different formatting, multiple columns, and a variety of page layouts.
- Create styles that include a combination of formats, such as indented paragraphs, bold text, or borders.
- Replace the formatting in an entire document, and a style in parts of a document with another style.
- Add comments and annotations to a document without changing the original text.
- Use revision marks so that intended changes can be seen easily - such changes can then be accepted or rejected.
- Create a glossary of text and graphics which can be inserted in any part of a document.
- Insert footnotes in any part of a document's page with automatic numbering.

- Remove selectively from the display screen the toolbar, the ruler, the scroll bars, and the status bar, so as to provide a larger working area which might appeal to some users.
- Correct your spelling with an extensive spell checker - you can even add special words to it.
- Check a document's grammar and style and customise the latter to suit your needs.
- Look up the meaning of words and find synonyms with the use of the thesaurus.
- Create tables in a document, which can contain text, numbers, pictures and objects - formatting can be applied to the whole, or individual parts of it.
- Add pictures to a document which were created in another application, scale them proportionally, or crop them to requirement.
- Ability to create objects, such as graphs, charts and equations, which can be modified, edited, moved and/or copied.
- Insert a frame around a paragraph, picture or object, then move the frame and its contents, or change its size.
- View documents in a variety of ways, preview a document before printing, print a document or print/view information about a document.
- Automated printing of envelopes, provided the printer's envelope feeder has been installed.
- Ability to organize documents by using outlines to structure text, modify such outlines, and create a table of contents.
- Use a find-file facility to search documents for a specified subject, ability to browse the text and graphics within such document files before opening them, and view information about them.
- On-line tutorials to help you with Word for Windows, and a much enhanced context sensitive Help command.
- Optional user's help to ease the change from WordPerfect to Word for Windows.
- Transparent importing of existing files produced by most versions of Microsoft and WordPerfect word processors, as well as worksheets and databases produced in Excel, Lotus 1-2-3, and dBase formats.

Icons and Toolbar:
Word for Windows supports numerous buttons which are to be found in the Toolbar, underneath the menu bar, at the top of the screen. These are colourful icons, or speed-keys, that give you mouse click access to the functions most often used in the program. The usual drop menus are still present but need only be used if a button does not exist to perform the required function.

To obtain a description of what an icon button can do when clicked, point to it and then press and hold down the left mouse button. This causes a description of the icon function to appear on the status bar at the bottom of the screen. If you don't want to continue with the selected function, drag the mouse pointer off the icon (while continuing to hold the left mouse button depressed), then release the mouse button.

A further selection of buttons are placed on the Ribbon, to be found immediately below the Toolbar. These buttons allow you to format and enhance your text in various ways. The Ribbon contains a font box which shows the font currently being used, and gives access to the rest of the installed fonts. Another button lets you change the font size, while others allow you to change the attributes of the font, such as italic and underline. Further buttons allow you to change justification of preselected text, or set different types of tabs.

Style and Templates:
Word differs in one basic way from DOS based word processors in that it uses styles to control the formatting of paragraphs and pages within a document, and templates to create a wide variety of different types of documents, such as memos, letters, reports, academic articles, and legal briefs. Templates are files that can contain text, graphics, formatting instructions, macros, and styles.

Once you get accustomed to using styles and templates, you will find it saves you an enormous amount of time with document formatting. Once a style is changed, the changes are reflected everywhere the style is used. You can even create a 'next' style to always follow a given style. Word for Windows comes with nearly 20 pre-defined templates. With these alone you should be able to create attractive and functional letters, memos, reports, books, etc., but you can also modify these in any way you like to make completely new templates for your documents.

Hardware Requirements

To install Word for Windows, you need an IBM AT compatible or PS/2 computer equipped with an 80286 or higher processor, at least 2MB of RAM and with Microsoft Windows 3.0 or higher, installed.

Installing the complete version of Word on such a machine requires about 15MB of hard disc space. Although it is possible to operate from the keyboard alone, the availability of a mouse is a must if you are going to benefit from the program's features and from Window's Graphical User Interface (GUI). After all, pointing and clicking (with the left mouse button) at an option on the screen to start an operation, or pointing and double-clicking at an icon to start a program, is a lot easier than having to learn several different key combinations. So if you can, install a mouse.

Installing Word for Windows

Installing Word on your computer's hard disc is made very easy with the use of the SETUP program on Disk 1. You need to run this program because part of its job is to convert compressed files from the distribution discs prior to copying them onto your hard disc; it then configures Windows to run Word.

Insert the Microsoft Word for Windows distribution disc #1 into drive A: and start the installation from the Program Manager of Windows, by clicking your mouse on **File**, followed by **Run** and typing

A:\setup

in the dialogue box, as shown below:

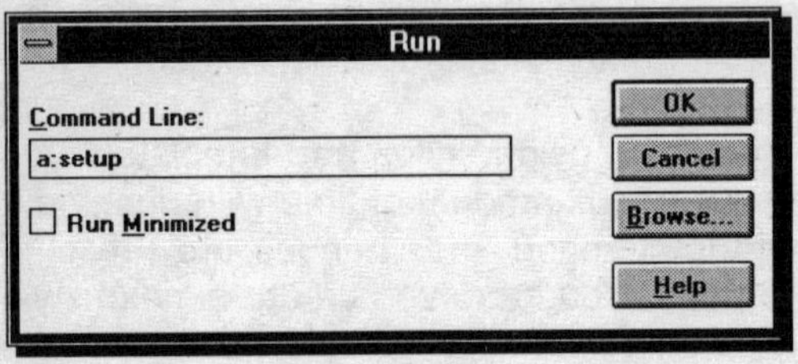

The first time you do this you will be asked to type your name on the initial screen produced. Word will generate a set of initials for you which may be used later, if you carry out document correction, for example. Word then initializes SETUP ready for the transfer of files and displays the following screen:

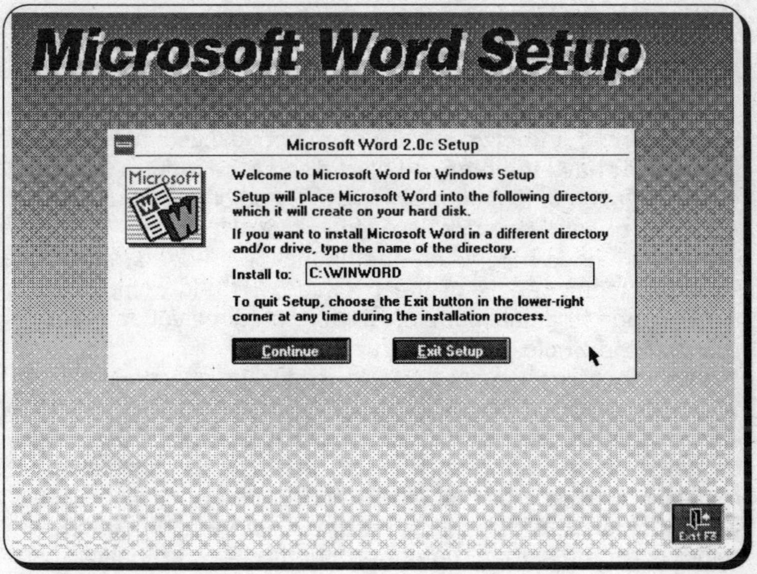

You could change the default directory, but we suggest you accept it by pressing the **Continue** button (or Alt+C). Setup creates the specified directory, and displays the screen below:

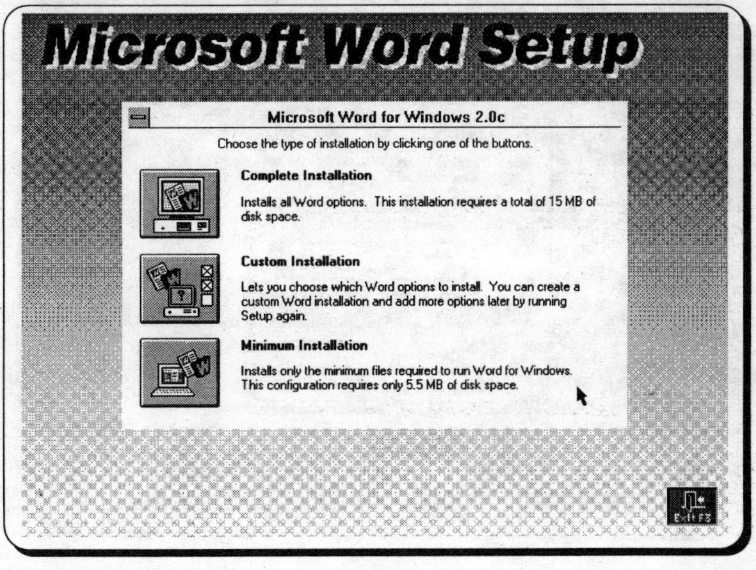

This is the main installation menu which will be repeated if you re-activate Setup. Note the amount of space required on the hard disc to install the program; 'complete installation' requires 15 MB and 'minimum installation' 5.5 MB - more if your hard disc is fragmented. In between, you can choose 'custom installation'. If you don't have the required hard-disc space, now is the time to exit installation and make some more by deleting unwanted files.

We suggest you use 'full installation', as the 'minimum installation' does not include the tutorials or, indeed, many other important components of the package. To add components of the package to a minimum installation, requires you to practically re-install the whole package again.

If you have enough hard disc space for the chosen installation, Word asks you if you want your AUTOEXEC.BAT file to be changed to add the WINWORD directory to your PATH and add a statement to run the SHARE utility. After answering the question one way or the other, Word starts installing itself on your hard disc. While this takes place, some useful information appears on the screen, namely about the Toolbar, buttons, spell and grammar checker, print merger, and help files, until another disc is required, as shown below:

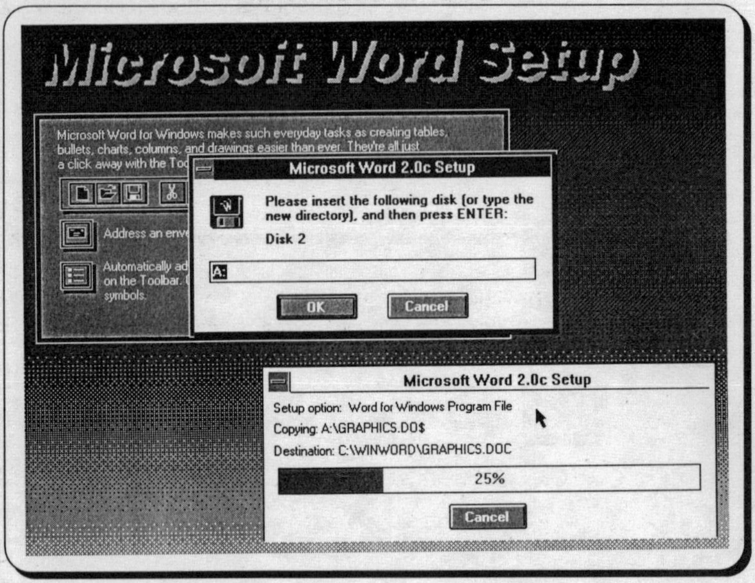

If the complete package is installed, 7 high density distribution disks will be used, and will take a good half-hour - the % bar indicates the number of files transferred rather than a percentage of total time required, so the first two discs take much longer than the rest.

If you are using Windows 3.0 you will be given the option to install Adobe Type Manager at the end of the process. Windows 3.1 has TrueType built in, so the ATM option is not needed. At this stage, you should get the following screen showing that the installation has been successful.

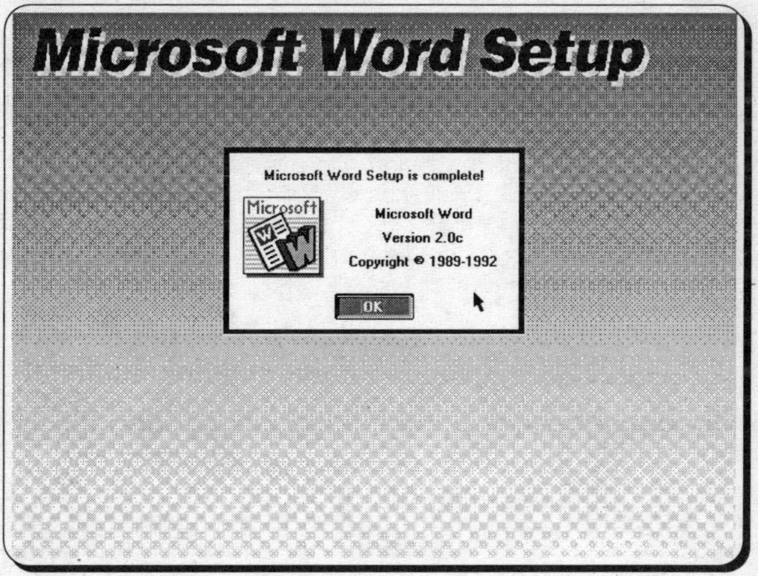

The program then adds icons to the Word for Windows Icon Group of the Windows Program Manager and is ready to be activated.

2. THE WORD ENVIRONMENT

Starting the Program

To start Word, as long as the WINWORD directory is included on your system path, you need only type the words **win winword** at the C:\> prompt. Otherwise you must specify the complete path to the directory in the command as follows:

```
win G:\WINWORD\winword
```

It is more usual however to start the program when Windows is already running as explained below.

Word Program Icons:

The install program opens a new group window in the Program Manager of Windows and names it **Word for Windows** as shown on the left. Two icons are placed in this window; the Microsoft Word for Windows icon and the Word Setup icon. It is this latter icon you should use to add portions of the package that you might not have installed to start with. You can leave this window intact, or move the two icons to one of your other Application Windows (by dragging them between the two windows with the left mouse button depressed) and then delete it with the **File** and **Delete** commands while the window is active.

Word is started in Windows by either double clicking the left mouse button on the above Word for Windows icon, or by double clicking on a Word document file (with the extension .doc) in the Windows File Manager. In this case the document will be loaded into Word at the same time.

Starting the Tutorials:

When the program is loaded, by double clicking the Word for Windows icon, you can start the tutorials by first clicking at the **Help** option in the menu bar, then choosing either **Getting Started** or **Learning Word**. Whichever one you choose, Word displays the screen shown on the next page.

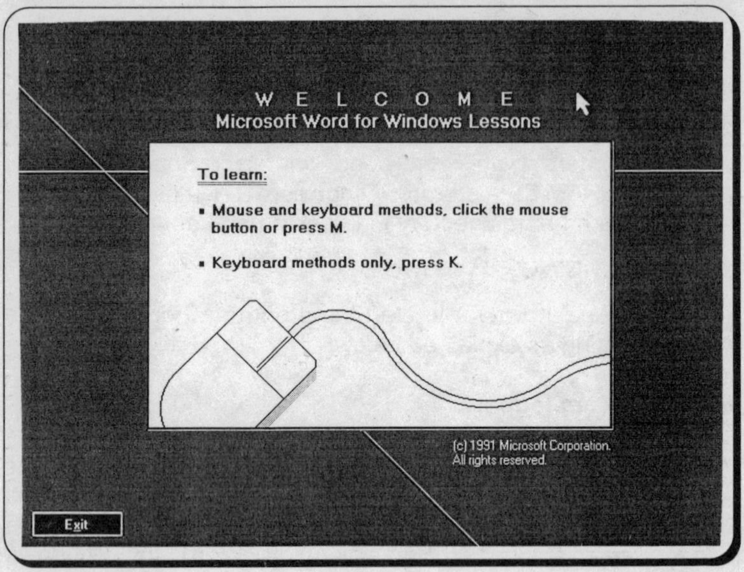

Following this screen, Word displays either the Getting Started screen, shown below, or the Learning Word Screen, shown on the next page, depending on which tutorial you chose.

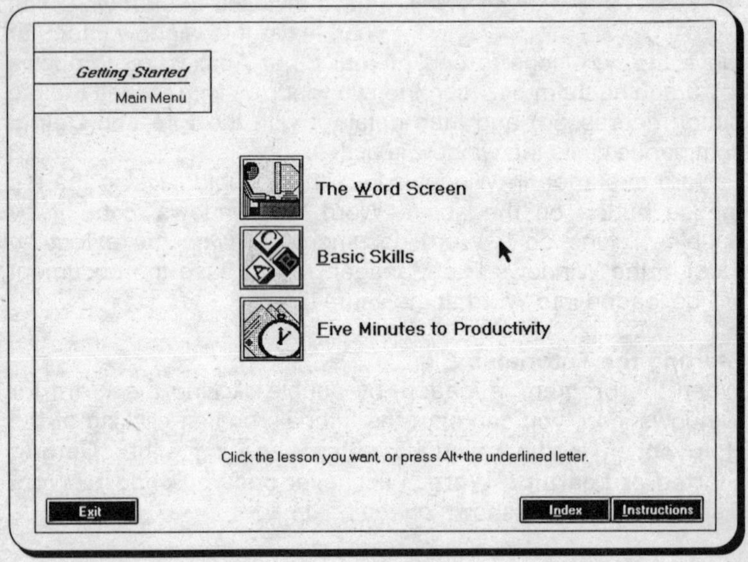

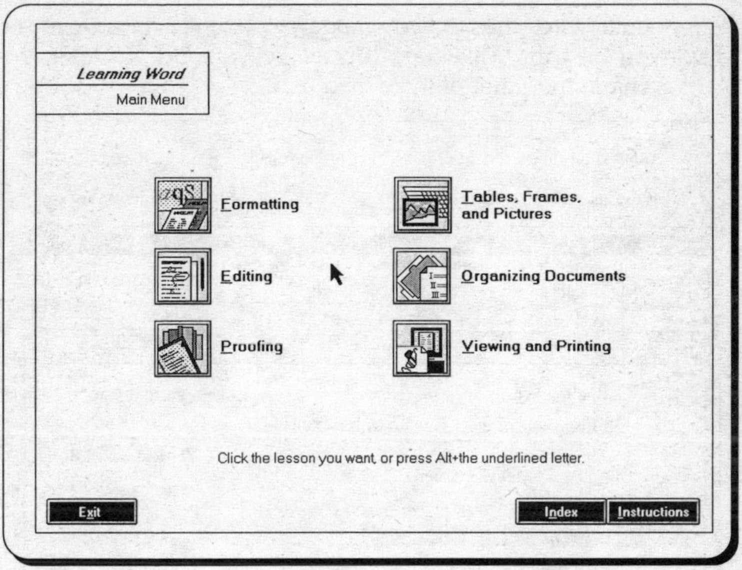

You can of course run through these tutorials as often as you like. When you have finished with a tutorial return to its Main menu screen and select the **Exit** button.

The Word Screen

The opening 'blank' screen of Word for Windows is shown on the next page. It is perhaps worth spending some time looking at the various parts that make up this screen, or window. Word follows the usual Microsoft Windows conventions and if you are familiar with these you can skip through this section. Otherwise a few minutes might be well spent here.

The window as shown takes up the full screen area available. If you click on the application restore button, the top one of the two restore buttons at the top right of the screen, you can make Word show in a smaller window. This can be useful when you are running several applications at the same time and you want to transfer between them with the mouse.

Note that the Word window, which in this case displays an empty document with the title 'Document1', has a solid 'Title bar', indicating that it is the active application window. Although multiple windows can be displayed simultaneously, you can only enter data into the active window (which will always be displayed on top). Title bars of non active windows appear a lighter shade than that of the active one.

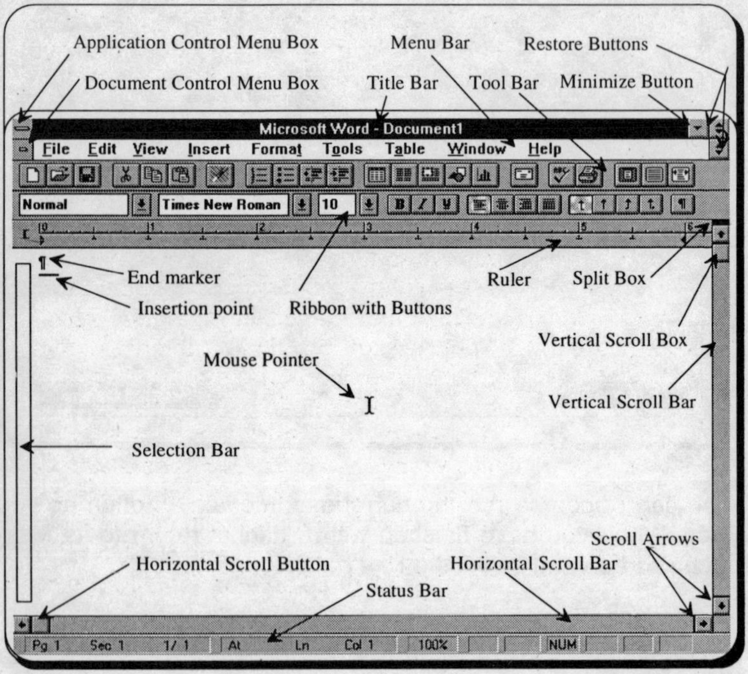

The Word screen is divided into several areas which have the following functions. These are described from the top of the screen down, working from left to right.

Area	***Function***
Control boxes	Clicking on the top control menu box, (upper left corner of the window), displays the pull-down Control menu which can be used to control the program window. It includes commands for re-sizing, moving, maximising, minimising, switching to another task, and closing the window. The lower menu box controls the current document window in the same manner.

Title bar	The bar at the top of a window which displays the application name and the name of the current document.
Menu bar	The bar below the Title bar which allows you to choose from several menu options. Clicking on a menu item displays the pull-down menu associated with that item.
Tool Bar	The bar below the Menu bar which contains buttons that give you mouse click access to the functions most often used in the program. These are grouped according to function, for example, the first three buttons deal with file manipulation, the next four with editing functions, etc.
Restore buttons	When clicked on, these buttons restore the active window to the position and size occupied before being maximised or minimised. The restore button is then replaced by a Maximise button, with a single up-pointing arrow, which can be used to set the window to its former size.
Minimise box	The button you point to and click to store an application as an icon (small symbol) at the bottom of the screen. Double clicking on such an icon will restore the screen and even maintain the cursor position.
Ribbon	The buttons on the Ribbon allow you to change the attributes of a font, such as italic and underline, and also to format text in various ways. The Ribbon contains three boxes; a style box, a font box and a size box which show which style, font and size of characters are currently being used. These boxes give access to other installed styles, fonts and character sizes.
Ruler	The area where you can see and set tabulation points and indents.

Split Box	The area to the extreme right of the Ruler which when dragged allows you to split the screen.
Scroll bars	The areas on the screen (extreme right and bottom of each window) that contain scroll boxes in vertical and horizontal bars. Clicking on these bars allows you to control the part of a document which is visible on the screen.
Scroll arrows	The arrowheads at each end of each scroll bar at which you can click to scroll the screen up and down one line, or left and right 10% of the screen, at a time.
Selection Bar	The area on the screen in the left margin of the Word window (marked here with a box for convenience), where the mouse pointer changes to an arrow that slants to the right. Clicking the left mouse once selects the current line, while clicking twice selects the current paragraph.
Status bar	The bottom line of the screen that displays information relating to your document, and in which a short description appears on what a button does when you point and click at it.

The Menu Bar Options:

Each menu bar option has associated with it a pull-down sub-menu. To activate the menu, either press the <Alt> key, which causes the first option of the menu (in this case the Document Control Menu box) to be highlighted, then use the right and left arrow keys to highlight any of the options in the menu, or use the mouse to point to an option. Pressing either the <Enter> key, or the left mouse button, reveals the pull-down sub-menu of the highlighted menu option. The sub-menu of the **File** option is shown on the next page.

Menu options can also be activated directly by pressing the <Alt> key followed by the underlined letter of the required option. Thus, pressing <Alt+F>, causes the pull-down **File** sub-menu to be displayed. You can use the up and down arrow keys to move the highlighted bar up and down a sub-menu, or the right and left arrow keys to move along the options in the

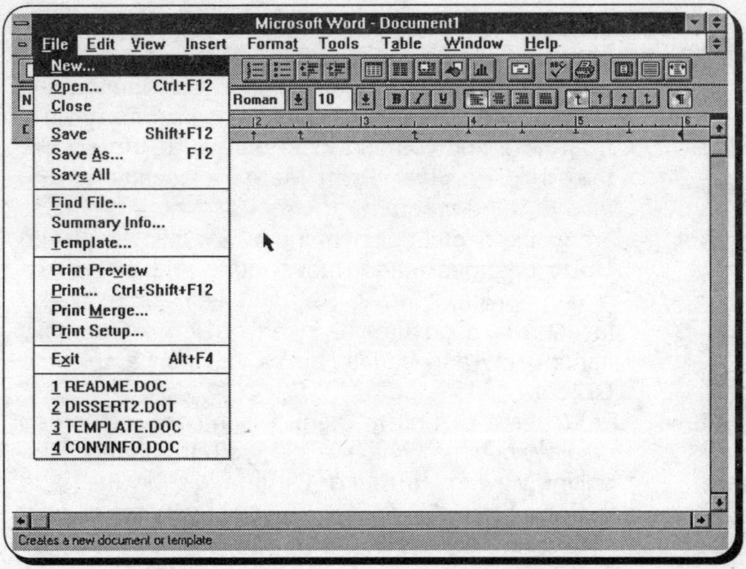

menu bar. Note that as you move up and down a sub-menu the status bar shows a brief description of the highlighted option. Pressing the <Enter> key selects the highlighted option or executes the highlighted command. Pressing the <Esc> key once, closes the pull-down sub-menu, while pressing the <Esc> key for a second time, closes the menu system.

Some of the sub-menu options can be accessed with 'quick key' combinations from the keyboard. Such combinations are shown on the drop-down menus, for example, <Shift+F12> is the quick key for the **Save** option in the **File** sub-menu. If a sub-menu option is not available, at any time, it will display in a grey colour. Some menu options only appear in Word when that tool is being used, but the following options remain constant.

For a more detailed description of each sub-menu item, either highlight it and read the text on the status bar, or use the on-line **Help** system, described later.

File Produces a pull-down menu of mainly file related tasks, such as creating a **New** document, the ability to **Open**, or **Close** files, and **Save** files with the same name, or **Save As** a different name. You can use the **Find File** option to search documents for a specified subject and to browse the text and graphics within documents before opening them, view **Summary Information** about them, and change the **Template** or its options. Finally, it is from here that you can **Print**, set-up a **Printer**, use the **Print Preview**, **Print Merge** a document, and also **Exit** the program.

Edit Produces a pull-down menu which allows you to **Undo** changes made, move, copy and delete text and graphics, **Find & Replace** text, jump to any location in a document, insert or define **Glossary** items, view and update **Links**, or open a selected **Object**.

View Produces a pull-down menu which contains screen display options which allow you to change the editing view to **Normal** or **Outline**, display the page in **Page Layout** (WYSIWYG - what you see is what you get), or **Draft** mode, control whether the **Toolbar**, **Ribbon**, or **Ruler** are displayed, show a list of **Headers/Footers**, open windows for viewing **Footnotes**, or **Annotations**, and determine the scale of the editing view by using the **Zoom** option.

Insert Produces a pull-down menu which allows you to insert **Breaks** to ends of pages, columns, or sections, add **Page Numbers** to a document, insert a **Footnote** reference at the cursor position, assign a name (**Bookmark**) to a section, or insert a comment and activate the **Annotation** pane. You can also insert the **Date and Time** into a document, insert a **Field** (instruction) for computed contents, or insert special characters with **Symbol**. Another set of options allow you to build an **Index Entry**, an **Index**, or a **Table of Contents**. Finally, you can insert the contents of a **File**, an empty **Frame** (or frame selected text), a **Picture**, or an **Object** into the active document.

Format Produces a pull-down menu which allows you to alter the appearance of text, both on the screen and when printed. Such features as font, size, colour, alignment, print spacing, justification, case and enhancements (bold, underlined and italic) are included. You can set and clear **Tabs**, change the **Border** of a document, or change the **Language** attributes of the selected language. It is from this menu that you can use **Styles** to apply, create, or change styles, change **Page Setup**, change the **Columns** format within a section, change a **Section Layout**, set the properties of a **Frame**, or change the scaling and size of a **Picture**.

Tools Produces a pull-down menu that gives access to **Spelling**, & **Grammar** checkers, the **Thesaurus**, and the **Hyphenation** option. It is from here that you can control the way **Bullets and Numbering** appear in paragraphs, use the **Create Envelope** option to print an envelope with the current document, toggle the **Revision Marks** on/off, **Compare Versions** of documents, or rearrange a part of your document in a specified order with the **Sorting** option. Other options, such as **Calculate**, allow you to check the arithmetic of a section in your document, **Repaginate** a document, **Record a Macro** (a set of instructions), or run, create or delete a **Macro**. Finally, **Option** allows you to change various categories of Word for Windows, such as view settings, general package settings, print settings, and save options.

Table Produces a pull-down menu that allows you to **Insert a Table** into your current document, **Delete Columns** from a table, **Merge** selected cells into a single cell, **Convert Text to a Table**, change **Row Height**, **Column Width**, insert a row into a table by using the **Split Table** option, and toggle the table **Gridlines** on/off.

Window Produces a menu to open a **New Window**, and control the display of existing open windows on the screen.

Help Activates the help menu which you can use to access the **Help Index**, select the **Getting Started** or Learning Word tutorials, or get information on **Product Support** and **WordPerfect** user help.

Dialogue Boxes:
Three periods after a sub-menu option or command, means that a dialogue box will open when the option or command is selected. A dialogue box is used for the insertion of additional information, such as the name of a file or path.

To see a dialogue box, press <Alt+F>, and select the **Open** option. The 'Open' dialogue box appears on the screen as follows:

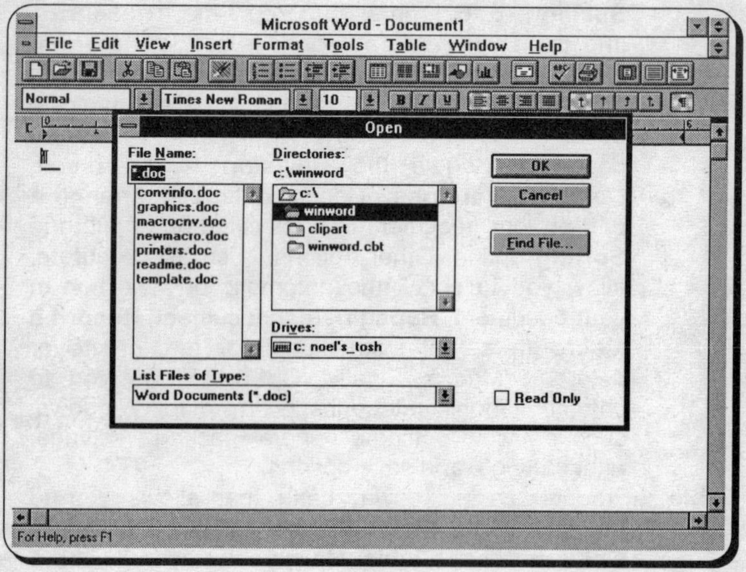

When a dialogue box opens, the easiest way to move around it is by clicking with the mouse, otherwise the <Tab> key can be used to move the cursor from one column in the box to another (<Shift+Tab> moves the cursor backwards), or alternatively you can move directly to a desired field by holding the <Alt> key down and pressing the underlined letter in the field name. Within a column of options you must use the arrow keys to move from one to another. Having selected an option or typed in information, you must press a command button such as the **OK** or **Cancel** button, or choose from additional options. To select the **OK** button with the mouse, simply point and click, while with the keyboard you must first press the <Tab> key until the dotted rectangle moves to the required button, and then press the <Enter> key. Pressing <Enter> at any time while a dialogue box is open, will cause the marked items to be selected and the box to be closed.

Some dialogue boxes contain List boxes which show a column of available choices. If there are more choices than can be seen in the area provided, use the scroll bars to reveal them. To select a single item from a List box, either double-click the item, or use the arrow keys to highlight the item and press <Enter>. Other dialogue boxes contain Option buttons with a list of mutually exclusive items. The default choice is marked with a black dot against its name, while unavailable options are dimmed. Other dialogue boxes contain Check boxes which offer a list of options you can switch on or off. Selected options show a cross in the box against the option name.

To cancel a dialogue box, either press the **Cancel** button, or press the <Esc> key. Pressing the <Esc> key in succession, closes one dialogue box at a time, and eventually aborts the menu option.

The Ribbon:

This is located below the Toolbar at the top of the Word for Windows screen and is divided into seven sections, as shown below. These can only be accessed by clicking on them with the left mouse button.

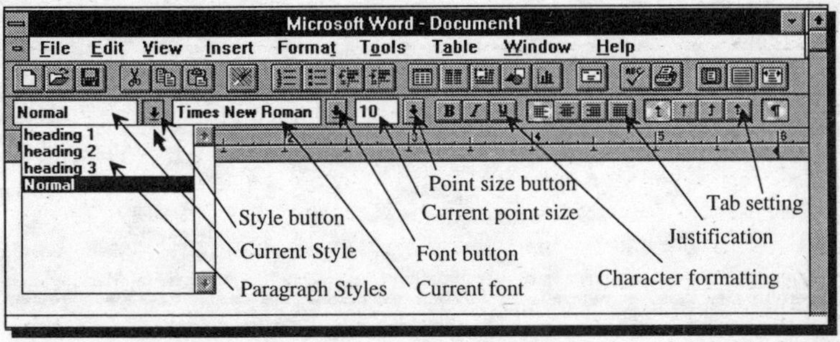

The Current Style window on the left of the Ribbon, shows the style of the current paragraph; the one containing the cursor. By clicking the down-arrow button next to it, a list of all the available styles, in the active template is produced (as shown).

Clicking on one of these will change the style of the current paragraph.

Next, and to the right of the Style button, is the Current font window which shows the current typeface. Clicking on the down-arrow button to the right of it allows you to change the typeface of any selected text.

The Current point size window shows the size of selected characters. This size can be changed by clicking on the down-arrow button next to it and selecting another size from the displayed list.

Following the Point size button are three Character formatting buttons which allow you to enhance selected text by emboldening, italicising, or underlining it. The next four buttons allow you to change the justification of a selected paragraph, while the next four buttons help you set the different types of tabulation points on your page.

The Status Bar:

This is located at the bottom of the Word window and is used to display statistics about the active document. For example, when a document is being opened, the Status bar displays for a short time its name and length in terms of total number of characters. Once a document is opened, the Status bar changes to the following:

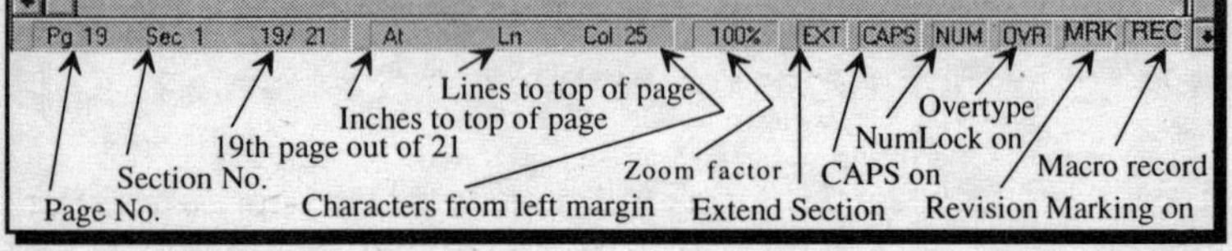

This shows the statistics of the document at the insertion point; here it is on Page 19, Section 1, 25 characters from the left margin. Also, the <CapsLock>, and <NumLock> keys are on. The OVR mode can be turned off by pressing the <Ins> key.

3. THE WINDOWS ENVIRONMENT

The Mouse Pointers

As with all other graphical based programs the use of a mouse makes many operations both easier and more fun to carry out.

Word has several different mouse pointers (similar to those found in Windows 3.1) which it uses for its various functions. These are all illustrated below. When the program is initially started up the first you will see is the hourglass, which turns into a large I-beam when the pointer is over your text editing area. As soon as the pointer is moved over the borders, menus or dialogue boxes it changes to an upward pointing hollow arrow. In the selection bar area, the pointer slants to the right.

The hourglass which displays when you are waiting while WinWord is performing a function.

The I-beam which appears in normal text areas of the screen.

The arrow which appears when the pointer is placed over menus, scrolling bars, and buttons.

The slanted arrow which appears when the pointer is placed in the selection bar area of text or a table.

The move arrow which appears when drag-moving text.

The frame arrow which you drag to create a frame.

The 4-Headed arrow used to move a frame.

The large 4-headed arrow which appears after choosing the **Control, Move/Size** command(s) for moving or sizing windows.

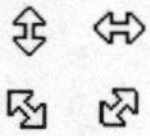

Double arrows which appear when over the border of a window, or the side of a frame, used to drag the side and alter the size of the window, or frame.

 The split box which appears when you select the **Control, Split** command, or the mouse pointer is on the split box in the vertical scroll bar.

 The vertical split arrow which appears when pointing on the vertical separation of cells in a table, and used to change the width of table columns.

 The vertical pointer which appears when pointing over a column in a table and used to select the column.

 The Help hand which appears in the help windows, and is used to access "hypertext" type links.

Manipulating Windows

Word for Windows allows the display of multiple windows, like any other Windows application. At some stage you may need to manipulate a series of windows, by selecting which one is to be active, by moving them so that you can see all the relevant parts, or indeed by re-sizing them. What follows is a short discussion on how to manipulate windows.

Changing the Active Window:

To select the active window amongst those displayed on the screen, point to it and click the left mouse button, or, if you are in full screen mode, choose the **Window** option of the main menu and select the appropriate number of the window you want to make the active one.

Moving Windows and Dialogue Boxes:

When you have multiple windows or dialogue boxes on the screen, you might want to move a particular one to a different part of the screen. This can be achieved with either the mouse or the keyboard, but not if the window occupies the full screen, for obvious reasons.

To move a window, or a dialogue box, with the mouse, point to the title bar and drag it (press the left button and keep it pressed while moving the mouse) until the shadow border is where you want it to be, then release the mouse button.

To move with the keyboard, press <Alt+Spacebar> to reveal the Application Control menu, or <Alt+–> to reveal the Document Control menu. Then, press **m** to select **Move** which causes a four-headed arrow to appear in the title bar and use the arrow keys to move the shadow border of the window to the required place. Press <Enter> to fix the window to its new position or <Esc> to cancel the relocation.

Sizing a Window:

You can change the size of a window with either the mouse or the keyboard. To size an active window with the mouse, move the window so that the side you want to change is visible, then move the mouse pointer to the edge of the window or corner so that it changes to a two-headed arrow, then drag the two-headed arrow in the direction you want that side or corner to move. Continue dragging until the shadow border is the size you require, then release the mouse button.

To size with the keyboard, press either <Alt+Spacebar> or <Alt+–> to reveal the Application Control menu or the Document Control menu, then press **s** to select **Size** which causes the four-headed arrow to appear. Now press the arrow key that corresponds to the edge you want to move, or if a corner, press the two arrow keys (one after the other) corresponding to the particular corner, which causes the pointer to change to a two-headed arrow. Press an appropriate arrow key in the direction you want that side or corner to move and continue to do so until the shadow border is the size you require, then press <Enter> to fix the new window size.

Minimising and Maximising Windows:

Word can be minimised into an icon at the bottom of the screen. This can be done either by using the mouse to click at the 'Minimise' button (the downward arrow in the upper-right corner of the window), or by pressing <Alt+Spacebar> or <Alt+–> to reveal the Application Control menu or the Document Control menu, and selecting **n** for **Minimise**.

To maximise a window so that it fills the entire screen, either click on the 'maximise' button (the upward arrow in the upper-right corner of the window), or press <Alt+Spacebar> or <Alt+–> to display the Application Control menu or the Document Control menu, and select **x** for **Maximise**.

An application which has been minimised or maximised can be returned to its original size and position on the screen by either double clicking on its icon to expand it to a window, or clicking on the double-headed button in the upper-right corner of the maximised window to reduce it to its former size. With the keyboard, press <Alt+Spacebar> to display the Application Control menu, or <Alt+–> to display the Document Control menu, and select **r** for **Restore**.

Closing a Window

Word itself, or a document window, can be closed at any time to save screen space and memory. To close a window either double click on the Control menu button (the large hyphen in the upper-left corner of the window, or press <Alt+–> and select **c** for **Close** from the Control menu.

If you have made any changes to a document since the last time you saved it, Word will warn you with the appearance of a dialogue box asking confirmation prior to closing it.

Windows Display Arrangement

In Windows' Program Manager, you can display multiple windows in both tiled and cascaded (overlapping) forms - the choice being a matter of balance between personal preference and the type of work you are doing at the time.

In Word for Windows, multiple documents are only displayed automatically in tile form, but you could rearrange them. To illustrate the point, select the **File, New** command twice; each time you select this command, the following dialogue box appears on the screen:

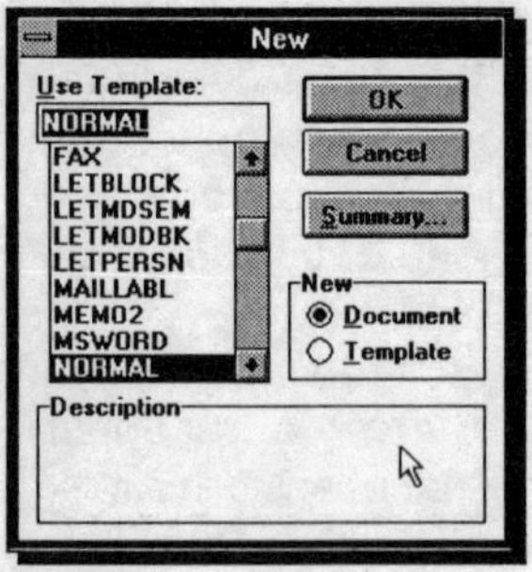

This 'New' dialogue box, which will be discussed in more detail later, is used to select the template to be used with a new document. In this case the default 'Normal' template is fine, therefore accept it by pressing <Enter>, or by clicking the **OK** button. When Document3 is displayed on screen, select the **Window, Arrange All** command. The three opened windows then rearrange themselves in tile form, as shown on the next page.

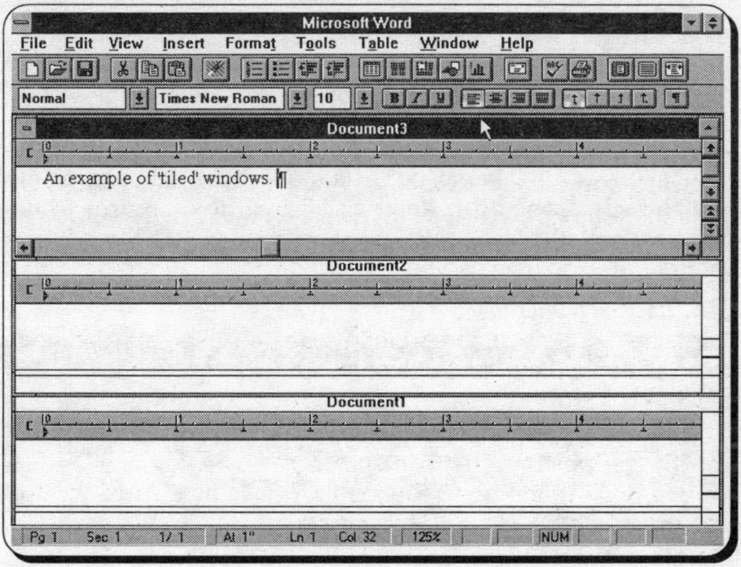

Now try to arrange these windows in cascade form by resizing them and moving them so they appear as follows:

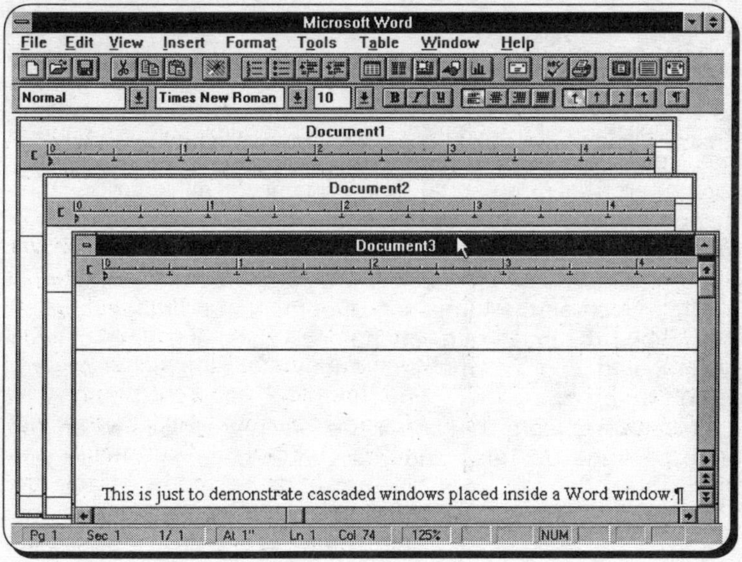

The Windows Control Panel

The Control Panel provides a quick and easy way to change the hardware and software settings of your system. For the sake of completeness we describe its use at this point.

Access to the Control Panel, from within Word, is from the Application Control Menu box, situated at the left end of the Title Bar. Selecting **Run**, then clicking on the **Control Panel** option opens the following window from which the various Control Panel options can be accessed.

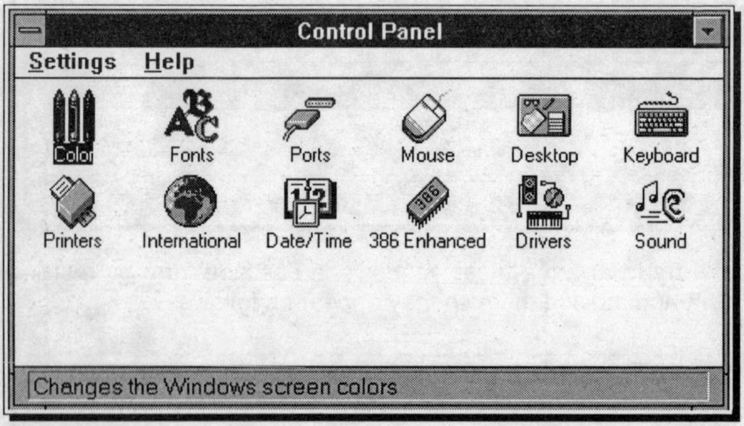

Double-clicking at the Control Panel icons allows you to change the display colours, change the display and printer fonts, specify parameters for any serial ports installed on your system, change the settings of your mouse, change the appearance of your display, specify resource allocations when running in 386 mode, install and configure your printer(s), specify international settings, such as the formatting of numbers and dates, change the keyboard repeat rate, change the date and time of your system, and specify whether Windows should beep when it detects an error.

All of these features control the environment in which the Word package operates and you should become familiar with them.

Adding a Printer:

Each time you choose to install a different printer, you'll have to activate the Control Panel as described in the previous section, and then double-click on the 'Printers' icon which will cause the following dialogue box to be opened.

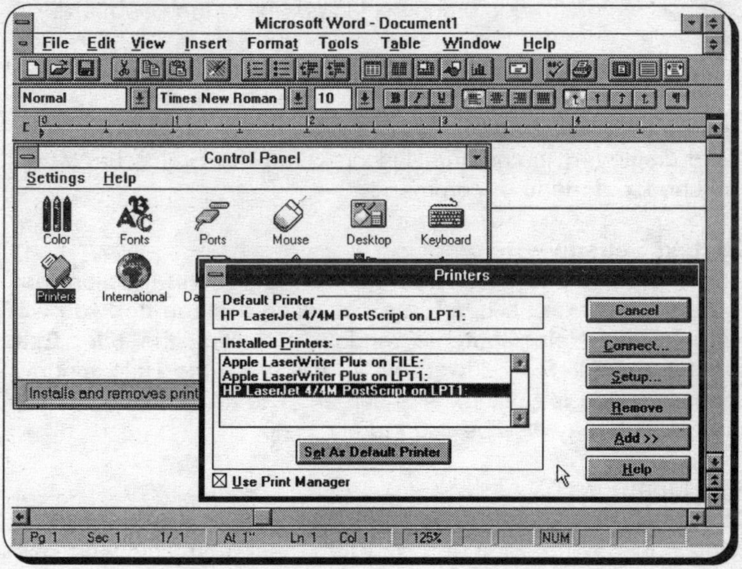

Selecting the **Add >>** button, causes Windows to display a list of supported printers from which you can choose the one you require. Windows will then ask you to insert a specific installation disc in drive A:, so that the correct driver can be copied on to your hard disc.

In the above screen, two printer drivers were installed; a PostScript Apple Laser Writer Plus, configured for output to a File, as well as via the parallel port LPT1, and an HP LaserJet 4/4M PostScript configured for output via the parallel port LPT1. The latter printer's name is highlighted and it also appears in the Default Printer box. Any of the other installed printers can be made the default by highlighting them and pressing the **Connect** button. The **Setup** button allows you to select the size of paper and orientation of printout (portrait or landscape).

Using Help in Word

Using the Microsoft Windows Help Program, Word provides on-line Help for every function. You can resize, move, tile, or cascade the Help window and the current document so that you can keep both of them displayed and you can even copy and edit text from the Help windows into a document by using Help's **Edit, Copy** command, to copy selected text to the Clipboard.

There are several ways to obtain on-line Help:

On-line Help Messages:
Word displays a command description in the Status bar when you choose a menu or command.

Context Sensitive Help:
Simply press **F1** to get instant help on any menu function that you are carrying out. If you are not using a menu box you will bring up the Help Contents window. Selecting the **File, Exit** command (<Alt+F> followed by X), will close the Help window and return you to your original screen. The <Alt+F4> quick key combination may also be used to exit Help.

Help Menu:
Choose **Help**, to display the menu, then choose **Help Index** to display the Word Help Index. From here you could choose **Instructions** or one of the listed options, such as Alphabetic Listing, and select the Help topic you want. With the keyboard, press <Tab> to select the desired topic and then press <Enter>.

Spend some time exploring the Help system. Most of the Word manual contents are in it; you just have to find them. A quick way would be to select Chapter Listing, read each screen of information and then click the >> button to move to the next page. Many Help topics contain cross-references to other related Help topics, which display in green. These are often known as 'hypertext' links, and clicking the hand pointer on them displays their content.

4. WORD DOCUMENT BASICS

In Chapter 2 we spent some time looking at the initial Word screen, shown on page 12. When the program is first used all the features default to those shown. It is quite possible to use Word in this mode, without changing any main settings, but as we work through the next two chapters we will explore some of the package's very powerful features, which will allow you to do much more than just the basics.

Entering Text:
Before going any further start Word, if necessary, and type the memo displayed below into a new document. The text may not be relevant to you, but it will give us a chance to illustrate some of Word's capabilities.

As you type in text, any time you want to force a new line, or paragraph, just press <Enter>. While typing within a paragraph, Word sorts out line lengths automatically, without you having to press any keys to move to a new line. This is known as 'word wrap'. If you make a mistake while typing, press the <BkSp> key enough times to erase the mistake and type the text again. At this stage, don't worry if the length of the lines below differ from those on your display.

If you want to type text indented from the left margin (like the last entry of the text below), use the <Tab> key before typing the information. Word has tab stops at every half inch by default. Formatting with tabs will be discussed later on.

MEMO TO PC USERS

Personal Computers
The microcomputers in the DP room are a mixture of IBM PS/2s (with 3.5" drives of 1.44MB capacity), IBM ATs (with 5.25" high density drives of 1.2MB capacity) and some IBM compatible machines, which are connected to various printers. As these only have 5.25" drives of 360kB capacity, before printing a document it must be saved on a 360kB format disc.

The computer you are using will have at least a 40MB hard disc on which a number of software programs have been installed. To make life easier, the hard disc is highly structured with each program installed in a separate directory. When the computer is first switched on, the following prompt is displayed:

    C:\>

Styles:
As you can see at the extreme left of the Ribbon, the Style Status box contains the word **Normal**. This means that all the text you have entered is, at the moment, shown in the Normal style which is one of the styles available in the NORMAL template. As mentioned previously, every document produced by Word has to use a template. By default the template NORMAL is used and at this stage we will not change this. The template contains, both the document page settings and a set of formatting instructions which can be rapidly applied to paragraphs within a document.

To demonstrate this, let's reformat our rather boring looking memo, but first, select the **Format, Page Setup** command, click the left mouse button at the Size and Orientation button of the displayed dialogue box, and change the page size from Letter (the standard American page size) to A4 (the standard British page size), as shown below, then press the **OK** button.

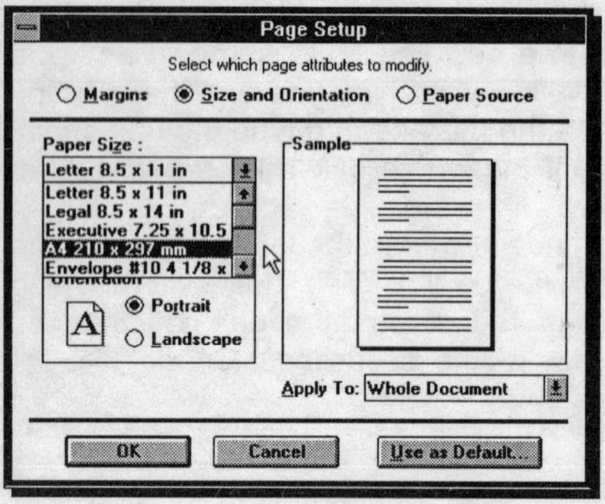

Next, place the cursor (insertion pointer) on the title line of the memo, left click the Style Status button, and select the **heading 1** style. The title line reformats instantly in bold, underlined and in Arial typeface of point size 12.

Now return to the memo and select the following styles. With the cursor in the second line of text select **heading 2** (reformats in bold, and Arial point size 12), then with the cursor in the first paragraph of text, select **indent small** (reformats in Helvetica point size 10) and repeat the latter style for the second paragraph of text. Your memo should look quite presentable now, as shown on the next page.

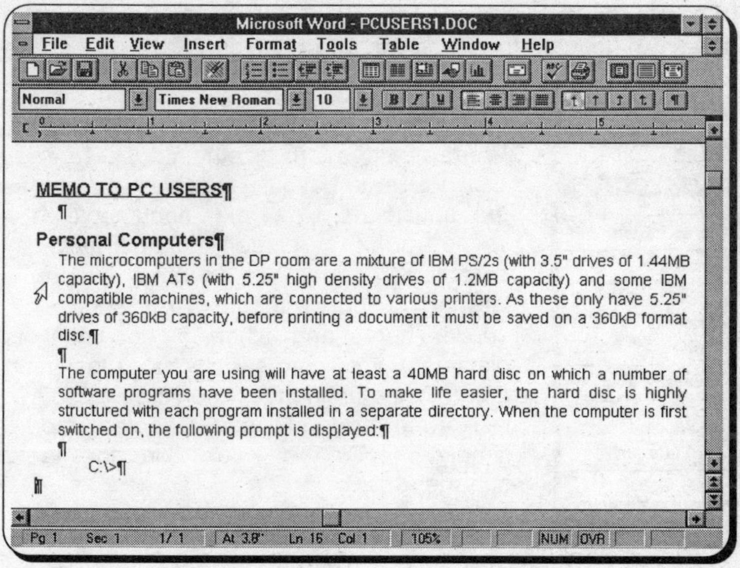

Moving Around a Document:

You can move the cursor around a document with the normal direction keys, and with the key combinations shown below:

To move	***Press***
Left one character	←
Right one character	→
Up one line	↑
Down one line	↓
Left one word	Ctrl+←
Right one word	Ctrl+→
Beginning of line	Home
End of line	End
Paragraph beginning	Ctrl+↑
Paragraph end	Ctrl+↓
Up one screen	PgUp
Down one screen	PgDn
Top of previous page	Ctrl+PgUp
Top of next page	Ctrl+PgDn
To beginning of file	Ctrl+Home
To end of file	Ctrl+End

In a multi-page document, use the **Edit**, **Go To** command (or press **F5**), to jump to a specified page number.

Document Screen Displays

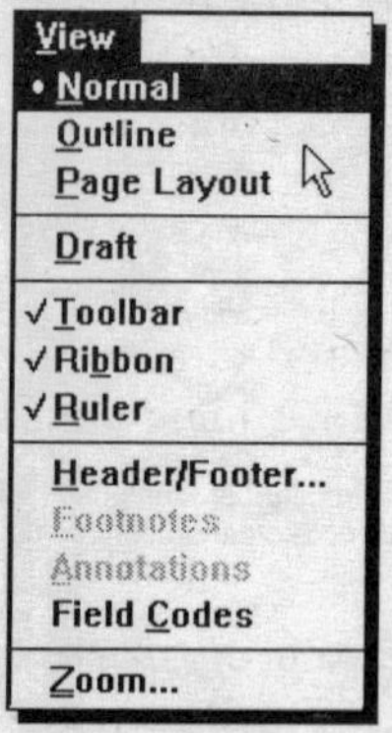

Word provides four display modes, Normal, Outline, Page Layout, and Draft, as well as the options to view your documents in a whole range of screen enlargements by selecting **Zoom**. You control all these viewing options with the **View** sub-menu, shown here, and when a document is displayed you can switch freely between them. When first loaded the screen displays in Normal mode. To select another mode, simply choose the mode from the **View** sub-menu.

Normal Mode:
Normal mode returns you to normal viewing from either Outline or Page Layout viewing mode.

Outline Mode:
Outline mode provides a collapsible view of a document, which enables you to see its organisation at a glance. You can display all the text in a file, or just the text that uses the paragraph styles you specify. Using the Outline mode, allows you to quickly rearrange large sections of text. Some people like to create an outline of their document first, consisting of all the headings, then to sort out the document structure and finally fill in the text. Outline mode is ideal for this type of working method.

Page Layout Mode:
Layout mode provides a WYSIWYG (What You See Is What You Get) view of a document. The text displays in the typefaces and point sizes you specify, and with the attributes specified, (alignment, indention, spacing, etc.).

All frames, tables, graphics, headers, footers, and footnotes appear on the screen as they will in the final printed document.

Draft mode:
Draft mode provides a less formatted view of a document. Text with attributes and enhancements appears underlined, and page breaks, headers, footers, or footnotes do not display. Tables and text display in their correct locations, but frames do not appear on the screen in their correct position, and pictures or objects are not displayed at all. You can edit the contents of a frame in Draft mode, but you cannot manipulate the frame itself.

The advantage of Draft mode is that you can edit a document very quickly, as the amount of computations required to display a document in Page Layout mode are reduced to a minimum, therefore speeding up the whole process.

Different Document Views

Word allows four main standard screen views of the document being worked on, plus two extra ones if you use the **Zoom to Fit Window** in either **Page Width** or **Whole Page** modes. All these screen options are accessed via the **View** sub-menu.

Standard View:
This shows the screen page in the same size as other Microsoft Windows applications with a **Zoom** magnification factor of 100%. In this view, if you are using a small font, you may need to use the horizontal scroll bar to view both the beginning and end of your lines. Other magnification factors are available, namely 200%, 75%, and 50%.

Custom View:
This view is fully editable and allows you to specify how much of the page will display. You control this view by selecting **View**, **Zoom** and setting the **Custom** level in the dialogue box as shown below:

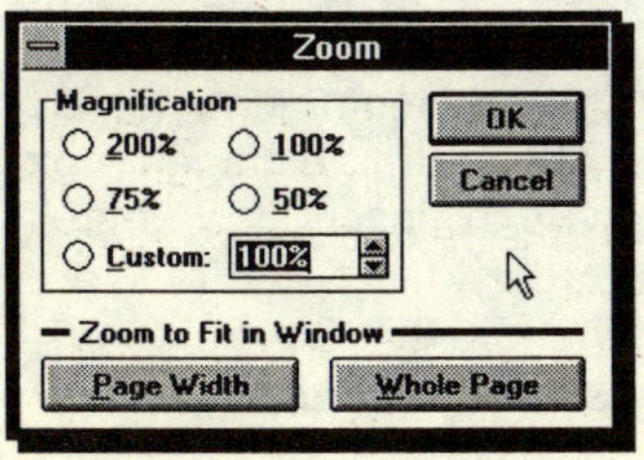

You can specify a percentage size between 25 and 200, where 100% represents the same as standard view. The default is set as 100%. Once you are happy about controlling this view it is the one you will probably be most comfortable working with.

The 200% view doubles the size of the standard view and allows you to zoom quickly to a portion of a page so that you can see fine details of your layout. This view is also fully editable and is most useful when using very small fonts.

Zoom To Fit In Window View:
There are two options under this view; 'Page Width', or 'Whole Page'. The first shrinks your document so that you can see the entire width of the page, including the margins, while the second shrinks your document so that an entire page can be displayed on the screen. The latter view displays correctly only in Page Layout mode. With it you may not be able to read all your document's text, but it can be very useful for checking on the layout of your pages, or for getting a rough overview of the document.

Display Screen Options:
You can choose to display certain parts of the Word window and hide other parts by selectively switching off the **Toolbar**, **Ribbon**, **Ruler**, **Header/Footer**, **Footnotes**, **Annotations**, and **Field Codes**. You can do this in all four modes and all views. If you turn off everything, you will be left with a screen which looks like a blank piece of paper, but for the **Menu bar**. You can select the parts of the Word window you want to display by clicking at the relevant **View** sub-menu options. By default, the **Toolbar**, **Ribbon**, and **Ruler** are switched on.

If you operate much with a clear screen, you will need to learn the keyboard shortcuts for commands (see Appendix A). These give you access to most of the more common menu commands without having to open the menu bars.

We leave it to you now to have fun exploring the different modes and views available in Word.

Changing Default Options

You can change the default options available to you in Word for Windows, by selecting the **Tools, Options** command (or by double-clicking on the Toolbar), to obtain the dialogue box shown on the next page, in which you can specify the default **View** options (what is displayed first), adjust the **General** Word settings, adjust the **Print** settings, change the **Save** options, and many others. Here, we only discuss the first four options.

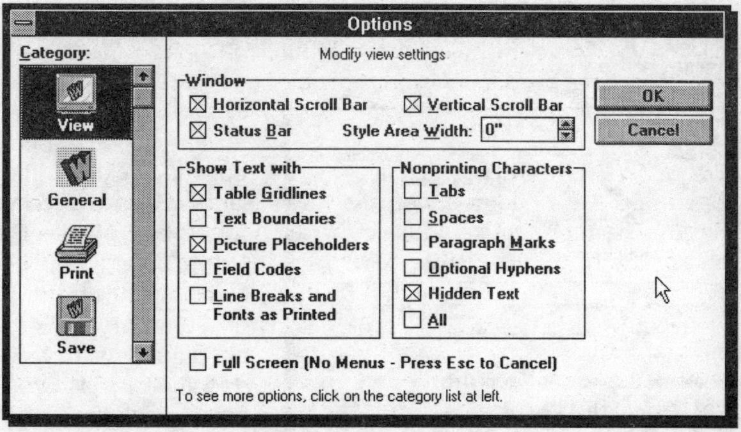

It is from this View dialogue box that you can change the way your current document window is displayed, the way text is shown, and whether non-printing characters, such as Tabs, Spaces, and Paragraph marks, are shown or not. Finally, if you select the **Full Screen** option, at the bottom of the dialogue box, you could achieve a temporary condition under which the screen looks like a blank piece of paper. When you need any of the displayed information which you chose through the **View** sub-menu, such as the **Toolbar** or the **Ribbon**, simply press <Esc>.

When you have finished with the 'View' options, you can select the 'General' button from the **Category** list, to obtain a similar dialogue box to the one above, but with a new set of options (shown on the left) available to you for adjustment.

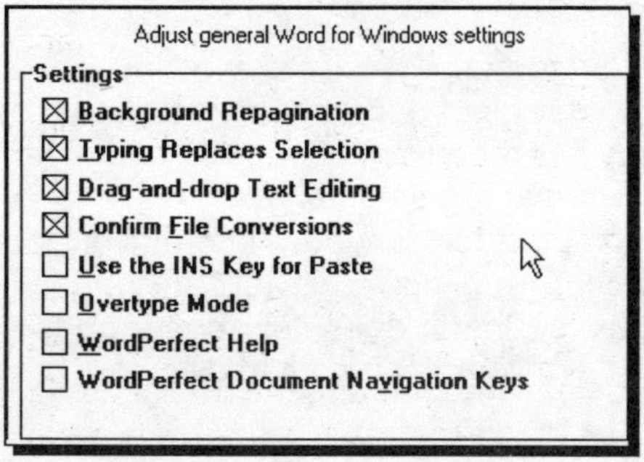

From here you can disable **Background Repagination**, disable the **Drag-and-drop Text Editing** option, select to **Use the INS Key for Paste**, or select the **Overtype Mode** as default, amongst other options.

To adjust the printing options, select the 'Print' button from the **Category** list, which causes the following set of options to be displayed:

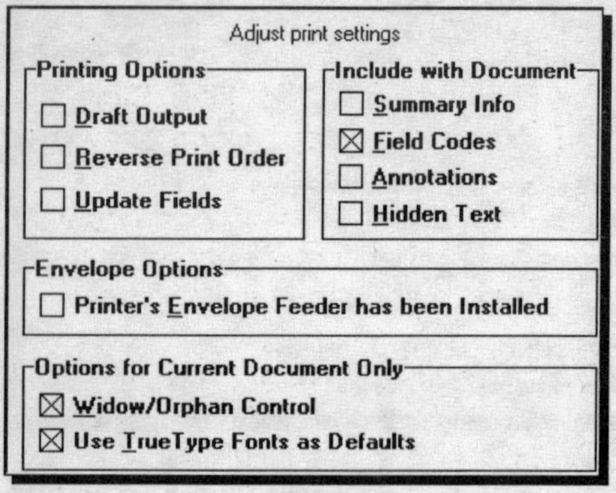

From here you can select various print options, including the **Draft Output** mode, and the **Reverse Print Order** mode, or select **Annotations** or **Summary Info** to be printed with your document. If you have installed the printer's envelope feeder, you could also print addresses on envelopes by selecting the **Envelope options**.

Selecting the 'Save' button from the Category list, displays the following set of options:

From here you can select the **Always Create Backup Copy** option for your work, or enable the **Automatic Save Every** so many minutes option. This last save option can be dangerous if you are working on a detailed document, change your mind and need to return to the original form, only to find it has been replaced. We find it far safer to manually save our work at regular intervals.

If you don't like to be prompted for summary information for your newly created document, you could disable this option from within this dialogue box, so that it does not appear on the screen when you first try to save your document to disc.

Saving to a File

To save a document to disc, use either the **File, Save** or **File, Save As** command. The **File, Save** command is used when a document has already been saved to disc in a named file - using the command automatically saves your work under the existing filename without prompting you. The **File, Save As** command is used when you want to save your document with a different name than the one you gave it already.

Using the **File, Save As** command (or the very first time you use the **File, Save** command when a document has no name). causes the following dialogue box to appear on your screen:

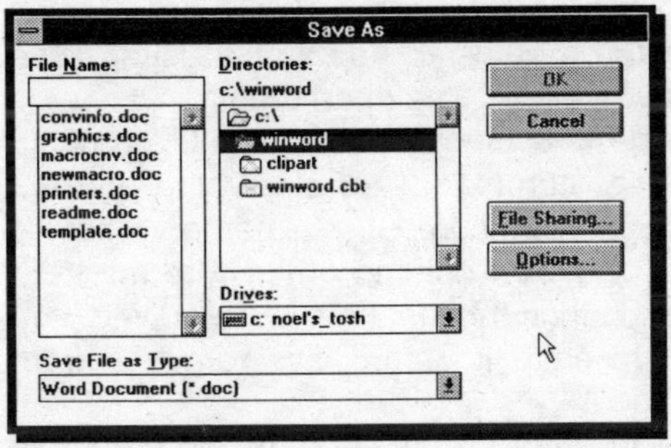

Note that the old document name is highlighted in the **File Name** field box and the program is waiting for you to type a new name. Any name you type (don't use more than 8 characters and don't bother to type the .doc extension as the program adds it automatically) will replace the existing document name.

You can select a drive other than the one displayed, by clicking the down arrow against the **Drives** field. To save your work currently in memory, move the cursor into the **File Name** box, and type PCUSERS1.

By using the **Save File as Type** button we could have saved the Document Template, or the Text Only parts of our work, or we could have saved our document in a variety of other formats, such as DOS Text, ASCII, Rich Text Format, or a number of WordPerfect, Word for Windows, and Word for DOS formats, as well as in Excel, Lotus 1-2-3, or dBase formats. All these different formats are saved with appropriate extensions which are recognised by the packages in question.

A useful feature in Word is the facility to add a document description to every file by selecting the **File, Summary Info** command. A box, as shown overleaf, opens for you to type additional information about your document.

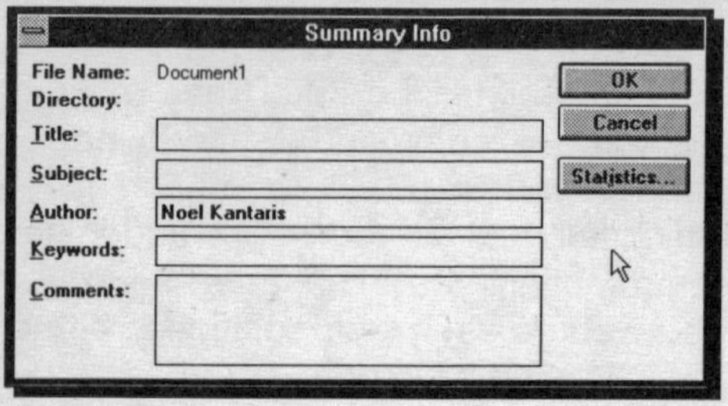

To do this on a more regular basis, make sure that the **Prompt for Summary Info** box in the Set Save Options dialogue box is selected and appears checked.

Closing a Document:

There are several ways to close a document in Word. Once you have saved it you can double click on the Document Control button at the left end of the menu bar; you would usually use this method when you have several files open together.

If you want to open a new, or another, document you could first use the **File, Close** command to close the current document (remove it from your computer's memory) before using either the **New** or the **Open** options of the **File** menu. If the document has changed since the last time it was saved, you will be given the option to save it before it is removed from memory.

If a document is not closed before a new document is opened, then both documents will be held in memory, but only one will be the current document. To find out which documents are held in memory, use the **Window** command to reveal the following drop down menu:

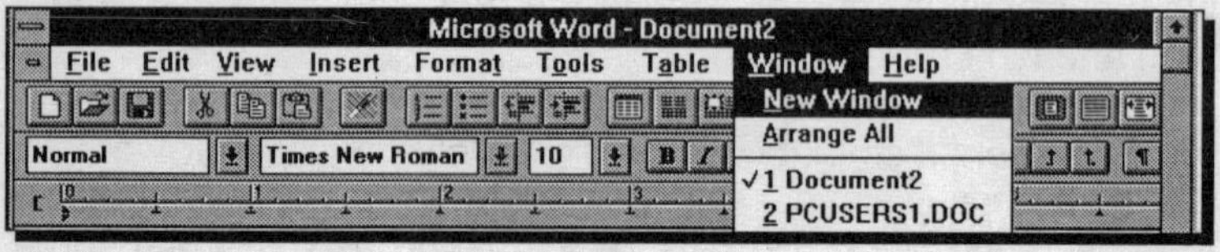

In this case, the first document in the list is the current document, and to make another document the current one, either type the document number, or point at its name and click the left mouse button.

To close a document which is not the current document, use the **Window** command, make it current, and then use the **File, Close** command.

5. EDITING YOUR DOCUMENTS

Document Editing

It will not be long, when using Word, before you will need to edit your document. This could include deleting unwanted words, correcting a mistake or adding extra text in the document. All these operations are very easy to carry out.

For small deletions, such as letters or words, the easiest method to adopt is the use of the <Del> or <BkSp> keys. With the <Del> key, position the cursor on the first letter you want to delete and press <Del>; the letter is deleted and the following text moves one space to the left. With the <BkSp> key, position the cursor immediately to the right of the character to be deleted and press <BkSp>; the cursor moves one space to the left pulling the rest of the line with it and overwriting the character to be deleted. Note that the difference between the two is that with <Del> the cursor does not move at all.

Word processing is usually carried out in the insert mode. Any characters typed will be inserted at the cursor location (insertion point) and the following text will be pushed to the right, and down, to make room. To insert blank lines in your text, place the cursor at the beginning of the line where the blank line is needed and press <Enter>. To remove the blank line, position the cursor at its leftmost end and press <Del>.

When larger scale editing is needed you have several alternatives with Word. You can use the **Cut, Copy** and **Paste** operations, after first 'selecting' the text to be altered. These functions are then available when the **Edit** sub-menu is activated. Instead of using the sub-menu you can click on Toolbar button alternatives for all the editing commands. This makes working with a mouse very much easier and quicker. A method, new to later version of Word is to use the 'drag' facility for copying or moving text.

Selecting Text:

The procedure in Word, as with most Windows based applications, is first to select the text to be altered before any operation, such as formatting or editing, can be carried out on it. Selected text is highlighted on the screen. This can be carried out in two main ways:

A. Using the keyboard, to select:

• A block of text.	Position the cursor on the first character to be selected and hold down the <Shift> key while using the arrow keys to highlight the required text, then release the <Shift> key.
• From the present cursor position to the end of the line.	Use <Shift+End>.
• From the present cursor position to the beginning of the line.	Use <Shift+Home>.
• From the present cursor position to the end of the document.	Use <Shift+Ctrl+End>.
• From the present cursor position to the beginning of the document.	Use <Shift+Ctrl+Home>.

B. With the mouse, to select:

• A block of text.	Press down the left mouse button at the beginning of the block and while holding it pressed, drag the cursor across the block so that the desired text is highlighted, then release the mouse button.
• A word.	Double-click at the word.

- A line. — Place the mouse pointer on the selection bar, just to the left of the line, and click once (for multiple lines, after selecting the first line, drag the pointer in the selection bar).
- A sentence. — Hold the <Ctrl> key down and click in the sentence.
- A paragraph. — Place the mouse pointer in the selection bar and double-click (for multiple paragraphs, after selecting the first paragraph, drag the pointer in the selection bar).
- The whole document. — Place the mouse pointer in the selection bar, hold the <Ctrl> key down and click once.

Try out both these methods and find out the one you are most comfortable with.

Copying Blocks of Text:

Once text has been selected it can be copied to another location in your present document, to another Word document, or even to another Windows application, via the clipboard. As with most of the editing and formatting operations there are several ways of doing this.

The first is by using the **Edit, Copy** command sequence from the menu, to copy the selected text to the Windows clipboard, moving the cursor to the start of where you want the copied text to be placed, and using the **Edit, Paste** command.

Another method uses the quick key combinations - <Ctrl+Ins> (or <Ctrl+C>) to copy and <Shift+Ins> (or <Ctrl+V>) to paste - once the text to be copied has been selected, which does not require the menu bar to be activated. As you get used to the Word package you will be able to save a lot of time by using quick key combinations.

A third method uses the 'Copy to clipboard' and 'Paste from clipboard' Toolbar buttons; you can of course only use this method with a mouse (see Appendix B for a detailed list of the buttons available in Word).

To copy the same text again to another location in the document, move the cursor to the new location and paste it there with any of these methods, as it is stored on the clipboard until it is replaced by the next Cut, or Copy, operation.

The last method for copying text is to first select the text, then hold both the <Ctrl> and <Shift> keys depressed, place the cursor at the start of where you want the copied text to be and press the right mouse button. The new text will insert itself where placed, even if the overstrike mode is in operation. Text copied by this method is not placed on the clipboard, so multiple copies are not possible, as with the other methods.

Moving Blocks of Text:

Selected text can be moved to any location in the same document. Use the **Edit, Cut,** command or <Shift+Del> (or <Ctrl+X>), or the 'Cut to clipboard' Toolbar button, move the cursor to the required new location and use the same **Paste** actions as described above. The moved text will be placed at the cursor location and will force any existing text to make room for it. This operation can be cancelled by simply pressing <Esc>. Once moved, multiple copies of the same text can be produced by other **Paste** operations.

Selected text can be moved by dragging the mouse with the left button held down. The drag pointer is an arrow with an attached square - the vertical dotted line showing the point of insertion.

Deleting Blocks of Text:

When text is deleted it is removed from the document, but placed on the clipboard until further text is either copied or deleted. With Word any selected text can be deleted by pressing **Edit, Cut,** or by pressing the <Del>, or <BkSp> keys. However, using **Edit, Cut**, allows you to use the **Edit, Paste** command, but using the <Del> or <BkSp> keys, does not.

The Undo Command:
As text is lost with the delete command you should use it with caution, but if you do make a mistake all is not lost as long as you act promptly. The **Edit, Undo** command (or <Alt+BkSp>) reverses your most recent editing or formatting commands.

Undo does not reverse any action once editing changes have been saved to file. Only editing done after the save can be reversed.

Finding and Changing Text:
Word allows you to search for specifically selected text, or character combinations, using the **Edit**, **Find & Replace** command. This opens a dialogue box as shown below.

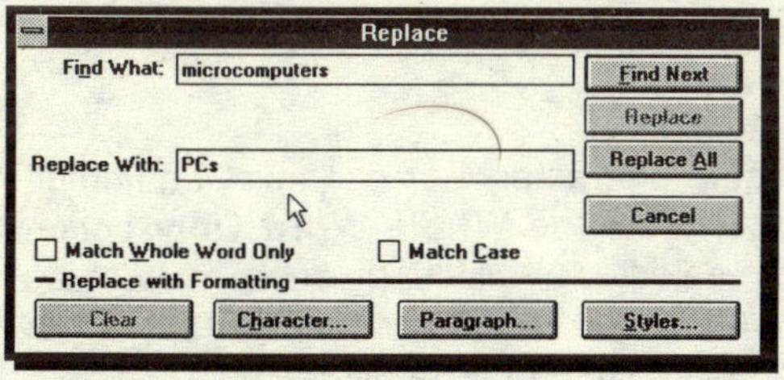

In the **Find** mode it will highlight each occurrence in turn so that you can carry out some action on it, such as change its font or appearance. In the **Replace** mode you specify what replacement is to be automatically carried out. For example, in a long article you may decide, as above, to replace every occurrence of the word 'microcomputers' with the word 'PCs'. Towards the bottom of the dialogue box, there are two check boxes with which you can match a whole word and/or the case of letters.

The buttons below the **Replace with Formatting** heading let you control how the search is carried out. You can force both the search and the replace operations to work with exact text case or attributes. For example, activating the **Character** button, lets you select font, font-size, style, and superscript/ subscript, while activating the **Paragraph** button lets you select alignment, indentation, and pagination.

Finally, activating the **Styles** button allows you to specify the search by style. By selecting **Style** you can search for, or replace, different paragraph styles. This can be useful if you develop a new style and want to change all the text of another style in a document to use it.

You can search for, and replace, tabs and hard returns, or a combination of both these and text. The list below gives the key combinations of special characters to type into the **Find** and **Replace With** boxes.

Specifying Text

Type	***To find or replace***
^^	A caret character
^?	A question mark
^–	An optional hyphen
^~	A nonbreaking hyphen
^d	A section mark, or hard page break
^n	A newline character
^p	A paragraph mark
^s	A nonbreaking space
^t	A tab character
^w	A white space
?	Any single character. For example, searching for nec?, while the **Whole Word Only** option is not selected, will find such words as necessary, neck, nectar, connect, etc. If the option is selected, only 'neck' will be found.

Quick Key Combinations:
To format text or paragraphs, use the following shortcut keys:

Character Formatting

Type	***Format***
Ctrl+B	Bold
Ctrl+D	Double underline
Ctrl+F	Font name - each press displays next available font
Ctrl+H	Hidden
Ctrl+I	Italic
Ctrl+K	Small capitals
Ctrl+N	New text
Ctrl+P	Point size - each press displays next available point size
Ctrl+Space	Remove character formatting from selected text

Ctrl+U	Underline
Ctrl+V	Colour - each press displays next available colour
Ctrl+W	Word underline
Ctrl+Z	Deleted text shown with strikethrough formatting

Paragraph Formatting

Type	***Format***
Ctrl+1	Single-spaced lines
Ctrl+2	Double-spaced lines
Ctrl+5	One-and-a-half-spaced lines
Ctrl+C	Centred lines
Ctrl+E	Close space before
Ctrl+J	Justify lines
Ctrl+L	Left-aligned lines
Ctrl+O	Open space before paragraph
Ctrl+R	Right-aligned lines
Ctrl+X	Remove paragraph formatting from selected text.

Page Breaks:

The program automatically inserts a 'soft' page break in a document when a page of typed text is full. To force a manual, or hard, page break in a document, either type Ctrl+<Enter> or use the **Insert**, **Break** command and select **Page Break** in the dialogue box, as shown below:

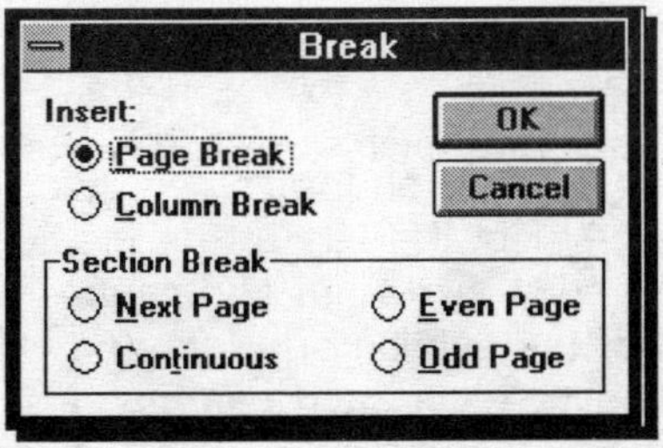

Pressing **OK** places a series of dots across the page to indicate the page break. You can delete manual page breaks by placing the cursor on the selection bar to the left of the page break mark, clicking once to highlight the line of dots, and pressing the <Del> key. You cannot delete the soft page breaks that the program inserts automatically.

Formatting Your Work

Formatting involves the appearance of individual characters or words, the line spacing and alignment of paragraphs, and the overall page layout of the entire document. These functions are carried out in Word in several different ways. Primary page layout and text formatting can be included in Style Sheets and Templates, which will be discussed in Chapter 6. Within any document, however, you can override Paragraph Style formats by applying text formatting and enhancements manually to selected text. If you cancel this manual formatting by selecting the text and selecting, **Undo Formatting** (Ctrl+Z) from the **Edit** sub-menu, the text will revert to its original format.

Formatting Text:

The fonts available in Word depend on the printer(s) you have set-up in Microsoft Windows and selected in Word with the **File**, **Print Setup** command. With Windows you can have fonts that display on your screen but that your printer cannot print, and vice versa (see next section).

If you select a printer font for which there is no exact screen font, then Word will select the nearest one that is available to display your work. Similarly, if the font selected is not available to your printer, Word will select the nearest one you do have available and will use that when printing. You might choose to do the latter, because you plan to print on a different printer from the one attached to your system. When you open your document on the computer that has the specified font, Word will display and print your document with the correct font.

Originally, the two header lines of the memo PCUSERS1, which we produced in the last chapter, were typed in the 12 point size Arial typeface, and the main text in 10 point size Helvetica. To change it into what appears on the screen dump displayed on the next page, first select the title of the memo and format it to bold, italics, 18 point size Arial and centre it between the margins, then select the subtitle and format it to bold, 14 point size Arial, and finally select each paragraph of the main body of the memo in turn, and format it to 12 point size Arial. All of this formatting can be achieved by using the buttons on the Ribbon (see section 'Paragraph Alignment').

If you can't access these font styles, it will probably be because your printer does not support them, in which case you will need to select other fonts that are supported. Save the result under the new filename PCUSERS2.

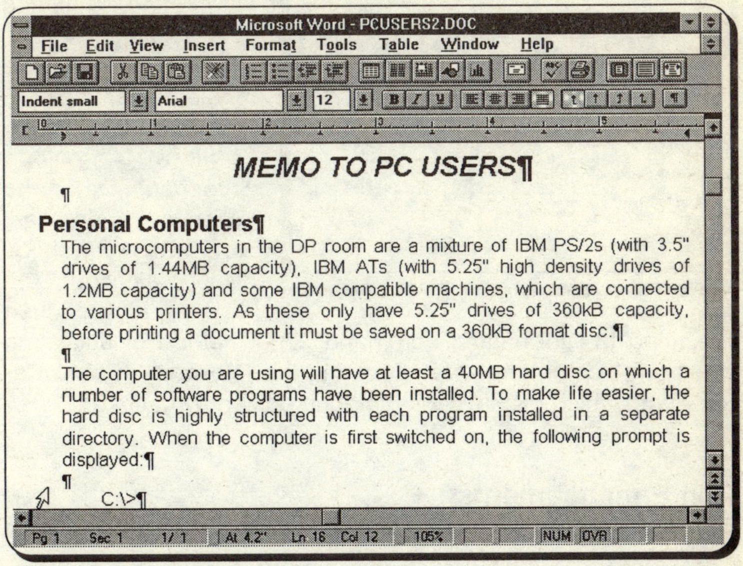

Some Font Basics:
A 'point' is a unit of measurement, approximately 1/72 of an inch, that determines the height of a character. There is another unit of character measurement called the 'pitch' which is the number of characters that can fit horizontally in one inch. The spacing of a font is either 'fixed' (monospaced) or 'proportional'. With fixed spacing, each character takes up exactly the same space, while proportionally spaced characters take up different spacing (an 'i' or a 't' take up less space than a 'u' or a 'w'). Thus the length of proportionally spaced text can vary depending on which letters it contains. However, numerals take up the same amount of space whether they have been specified as fixed or proportional.

Which fonts you choose is largely dependent on your printer, as mentioned previously. Windows 3.1 makes available several 'TrueType' fonts which can be used by Windows applications, such as Word. TrueType fonts are scaleable to any point size and look exactly the same on the screen as they do when printed.

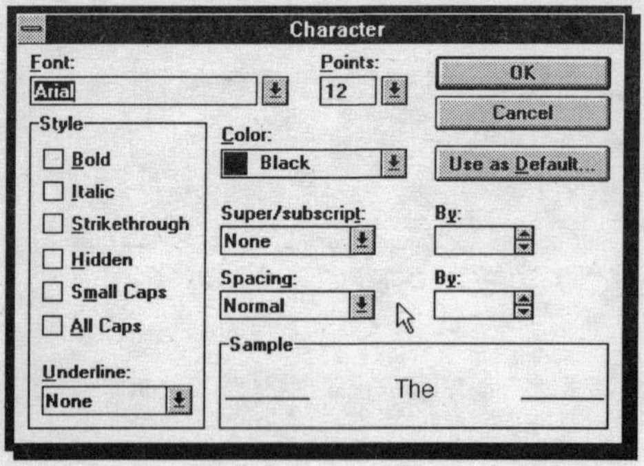

In Word all manual formatting, including the selection of font, point size, style (bold, italic, strike-through, hidden and capitals), colour, super/subscript, and various underlines, are carried out by first selecting the text and then executing the formatting command. One method of activating formatting commands is through the **Format**, **Character** command which displays the dialogue box shown above.

Text Enhancements

Word defines a paragraph, as any text which is followed by a paragraph mark, which is created by pressing the <Enter> key. So single line titles, as well as long typed text, can form paragraphs. The paragraph symbol is only visible if you have selected it from the Ribbon.

Paragraph Alignment:

Word allows you to align a paragraph at the left margin (the default), at the right margin, centred between both margins, or justified between both margins. As with most operations there are several ways to perform alignment in Word. These are as follows:

a. Using buttons on the **Ribbon**,
b. Using the **Format**, **Paragraph** menu command, or
c. Using keyboard short cuts, when available.

On the next page, we show the text alignment commands using all three methods.

Buttons on Ribbon	***Paragraph Alignment***	***Keystrokes***
	Left	<Ctrl+L>
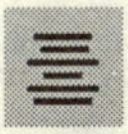	Centre	<Ctrl+C>
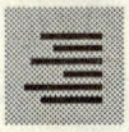	Right	<Ctrl+R>
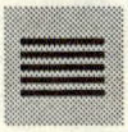	Justify	<Ctrl+J>

The display below shows the dialogue box resulting from using the **Format, Paragraph** command.

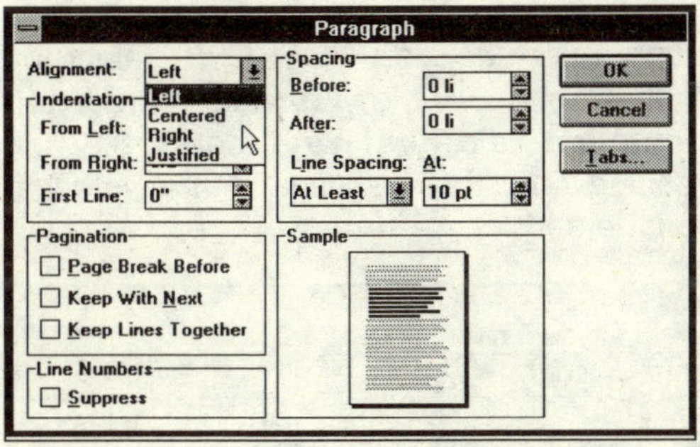

Whichever of the above methods is used, formatting can take place either before or after the text is entered. If formatting is selected first, then text will type in the chosen format until a further formatting command is given. If this method is used, or you choose to operate Word in clear-screen view mode, then the keyboard short cuts will be the fastest method. If, on the other hand, you choose to enter text and then format it afterwards, you must select the text to be formatted (by highlighting it) before you activate a formatting command.

Paragraph Spacing:

A paragraph can be displayed on screen or printed on paper in single-line, 1½-line, or double-line spacing, or you can set the spacing to any value you want with the At Least option and then specify what interval you want, as shown on the next page.

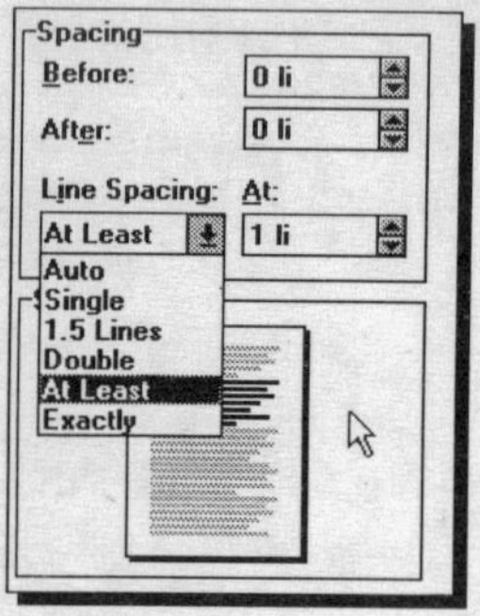

All alignment and spacing options can easily be selected from the **Paragraph** dialogue box of the **Format** menu command. When setting customised alignment indentations you have the choice of 4 units to work with, inches, centimetres, points or picas. These can be selected from the 'General' **Category** list of the **Tools**, **Options** sub-menu.

Indenting Text:

Most documents will require some form of paragraph indenting. An indent is the space between the margin and the edge of the text in the paragraph. When an indent is set (on the left or right side of the page), any justification on that side of the page sets at the indent, not the page border.

To illustrate indentation, open the file PCUSERS2, select the first paragraph, and then choose the **Format**, **Paragraph** command. In the **Indentation** field **First Line**, select 0.3", as shown below. On pressing **OK**, the first line of the selected paragraph is displayed indented.

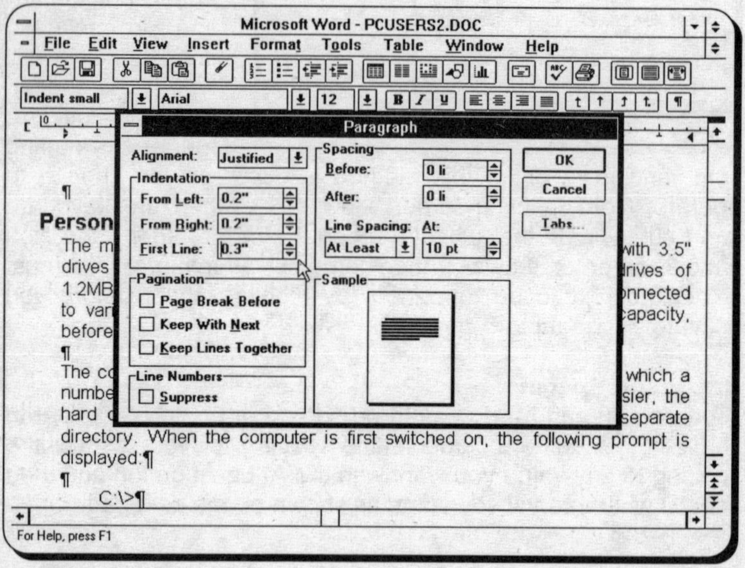

Hanging Indents:

The **Indentation** option of the **Format**, **Paragraph** command, can be used to create 'hanging' indents, where all the lines in a paragraph, including any text on the first line that follows a tab, are indented by a specified amount. This is often used in lists to emphasise certain points.

To illustrate the method, use the PCUSERS1 file and add at the end of it, after the 'C:\>' prompt, the text shown below. After you have typed it in, save the enlarged memo as PCUSERS3, before going on with formatting the new information. This is done as a precaution in case anything goes wrong with the formatting - it is sometimes much easier to reload a saved file (using the **File, Open** command), than it is to try to unscramble a wrongly formatted document!

C:\>

To find out what is on your hard disc, type

DIR (and press the <Enter> key)

which will produce a list of all the filenames on the 'Root' directory (the one with the C:\> prompt) - directories are displayed with their names in angle brackets, for example, <DOS>. If your hard disc is structured correctly, then each program package would have been installed in a separate directory. For example:

Name Description

123R24 Holds the LOTUS 1-2-3 Release 2.4 spreadsheet package.

QB45 Holds the Microsoft Quick Basic version 4.5 suite of programs which allow you to write and compile fully structured Basic programs. It is one of the best versions of non-visual Basic available.

Windows Holds the Windows suite of programs that controls your Windows environment.

Now select the text in the last 4 paragraphs above, choose the **Format**, **Paragraph** command, and type the figures shown here, in the three fields of the **Indentation** option of the displayed dialogue box.

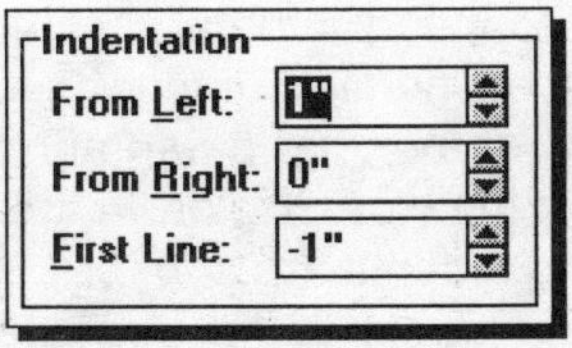

After selecting **OK** the text formats as shown overleaf, but it is still highlighted. To remove the highlighting, click the mouse button on the page. The second and following lines of the third paragraph selected, should appear indented 1 inch from the left margin.

To find out what is on your hard disc, type

DIR (and press the <Enter> key)

which will produce a list of all the filenames on the 'Root' directory (the one with the C:\> prompt) - directories are displayed with their names in angle brackets, for example, <DOS>. If your hard disc is structured correctly, then each program package would have been installed in a separate directory. For example:

Name Description

123R24 Holds the LOTUS 1-2-3 Release 2.4 spreadsheet package.

QB45 Holds the Microsoft Quick Basic version 4.5 suite of programs which allow you to write and compile fully structured Basic programs. It is one of the best versions of non-visual Basic available.

Windows Holds the Windows suite of programs that controls your Windows environment.

This is still not very inspiring, so to complete the effect we will edit the first lines of each paragraph, to end up with the display below.

To find out what is on your hard disc, type

DIR (and press the <Enter> key)

which will produce a list of all the filenames on the 'Root' directory (the one with the C:\> prompt) - directories are displayed with their names in angle brackets, for example, <DOS>. If your hard disc is structured correctly, then each program package would have been installed in a separate directory. For example:

Name	Description
123R24	Holds the LOTUS 1-2-3 Release 2.4 spreadsheet package.
QB45	Holds the Microsoft Quick Basic version 4.5 suite of programs which allow you to write and compile fully structured Basic programs. It is one of the best versions of non-visual Basic available.
Windows	Holds the Windows suite of programs that controls your Windows environment.

Place the cursor in front of the word 'Description' in paragraph 4 and press the <Tab> key once. This places the start of the word in the same column as the indented text of the third paragraph. To complete the effect place tabs before the word 'Holds' in the next three paragraphs, until your hanging indents are correct.

This may seem like a complicated rigmarole to go through each time you want the hanging indent effect, but with Word you will eventually set up all your indents, etc., in templates. Then all you do is click in a paragraph to produce them.

When you finish formatting the document, save it under its current filename with the **File, Save** command (<Ctrl+S>). This command does not display a dialogue box, so you use it when you do not need to make any changes to the saving operation.

Inserting Bullets:

Bullets are small characters you can insert, anywhere you like, in the text of your document to improve visual impact. In Word there are several choices for displaying lists with bullets or numbers. These are made available through the **Tools**, **Bullets and Numbering** command, which displays the following dialogue box:

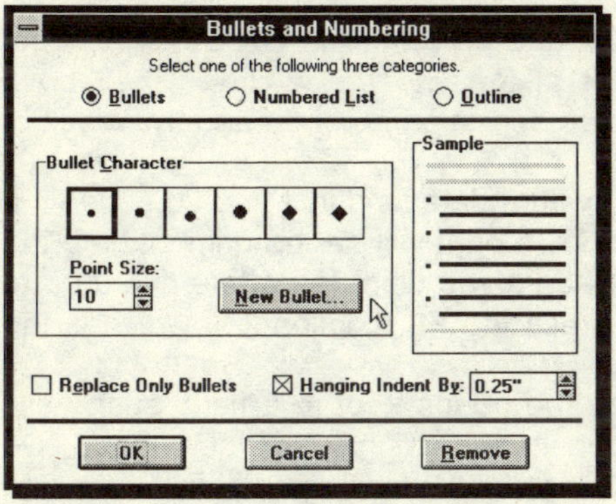

You can choose any of the bullets shown here, or you could press the **New Bullet** button to select any character from the Symbol typeface or other available typefaces. If you select the **Numbered List** option, a similar dialogue box is displayed, giving you a choice of several numbering systems.

Once inserted, you can copy, move or cut a bulleted line in the same way as any other text. However, you can not use the <BkSp> or <Del> keys to delete a bullet.

Inserting Date and Time:

You can insert today's date, the date the current document was created or was last revised, or a date or time that reflects the current system date and time into a document. Therefore, the date can be a date that changes, or a date that always stays the same. In either case, the date is inserted in a date field.

To insert a date field in your document, place the cursor where you want to insert the date, select the **Insert**, **Date and Time** command and choose one of the displayed date formats which suits you from the dialogue box shown overleaf.

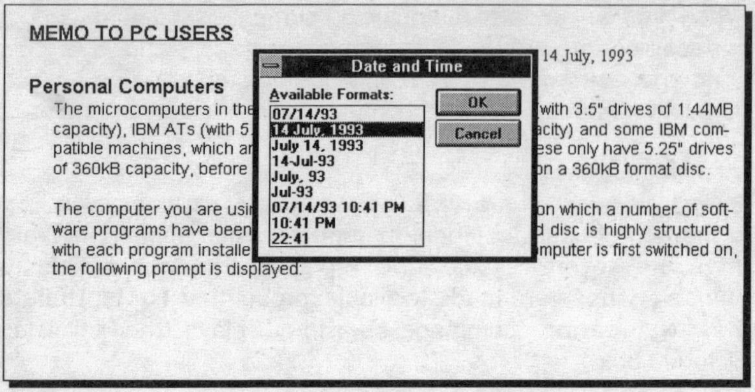

Highlighting '14 July, 1993' and pressing the **OK** button, inserts the date in our document at the chosen position. The above screen is a composite of the operation required and the result of that operation.

If you save a document with a date field in it and you open it a few days later, the date shown on it will be the original date the document was created. Should you want to update this date to the current date, simply press the **F9** function key which is the UPDATE FIELD key.

Word can either display the codes kept in a field, such as a date field, or the field results. To toggle between these two displays, place the insertion pointer anywhere within a field and press <Shift+F9>. If we do this in our case with the date field, we will get:

{TIME \@ "d, MMMM, yyyy"}

The reason for this facility is that you might want to mix two different types of formats, so the opportunity is presented for you to edit the code within a field.

If you do have such a need, and you have not inserted a date yet in your document, then use the **Insert, Field** command, select the type of field your want to create from the list on the displayed dialogue box - in this case Date. The word 'Date' appears in the Field Code box at the bottom of the dialogue box. At this point place the insertion pointer in the Field Code box after the word 'Date' and type the field code shown on the next page.

On pressing the **OK** button, the field result is displayed in your document. Again, the display below is a composite of what you do and what you get as a result of that action.

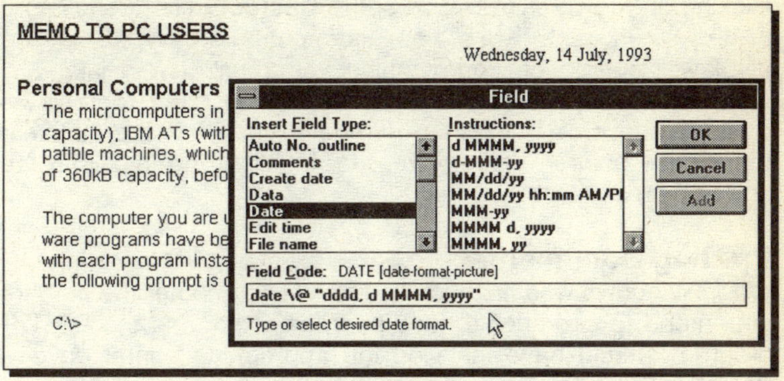

Inserting Annotations:

Another powerful feature of Word is the facility to annotate a document. These act like electronic labels - initialled comments by the people who might have an input to a document, as shown below:

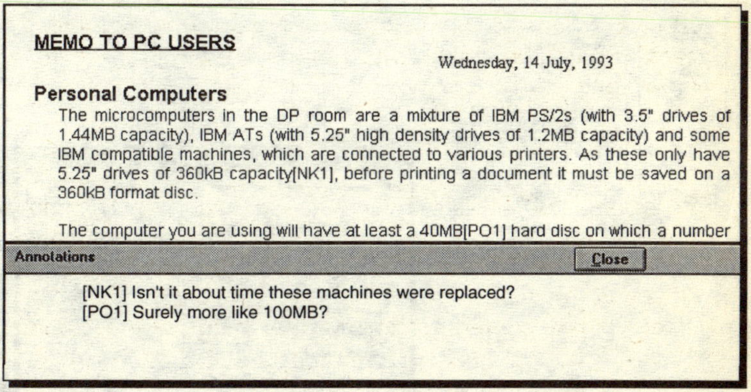

The initials of each person who views, and edits, the same document are used to mark the place in the text where an annotation is required. A separate annotation pane holds the actual comments.

To add annotations to a document, place the cursor at the place you want to add a comment, then use the **Insert**, **Annotation** command. Your initials (taken from the 'User Info' dialogue box, obtained by selecting the **Tools, Options,** command and clicking on the **User Info** icon of the **Category** list) are inserted in the main text, while your comments are typed in the displayed 'annotation' pane, against your numbered initials.

To open an annotation pane, when you need to read its contents, double click on the numbered initials in the text with the mouse pointer. To remove one, highlight the initials in the text and press <Del>.

Printing Documents

When Windows was first installed on your computer the printers you intend to use should have been selected, and the SETUP program should have installed the appropriate printer drivers. Before printing for the first time, you would be wise to ensure that your printer is in fact properly installed.

To do this open the Window's Control Panel, as described at the end of Chapter 3 and double click on the 'Printers' icon. This will open the **Printers** box shown below:

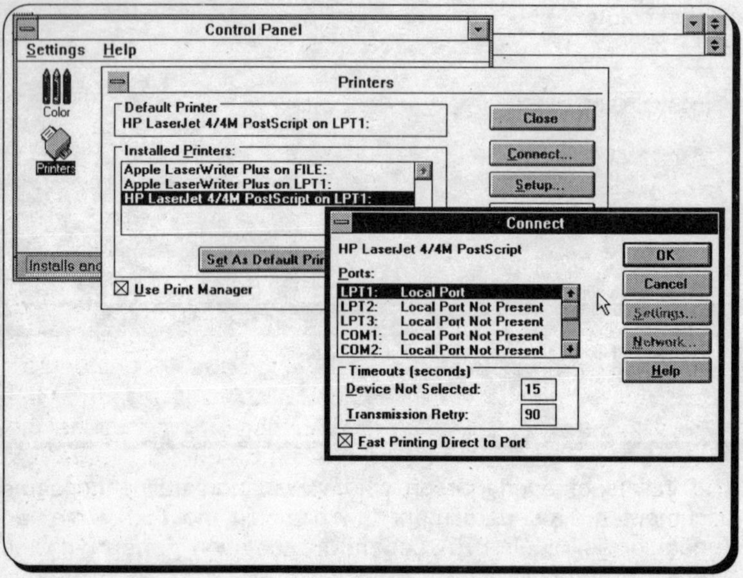

Here, two printer drivers have been installed; an HP LaserJet 4/4M PostScript printer as the 'default' printer configured to output via the parallel port LPT1, and an Apple Laser Writer Plus, configured to either print to a printer via the parallel port LPT1, or to a disc file. Your selections may, obviously, not be the same.

Best printed output results can only be obtained when using a laser printer. So, if you want to produce high-quality documents, and you have access to a laser printer (even if it is not connected to your computer and does not itself have access to Word), then install the laser printer as an additional printer to be used with Windows and configure it to print to 'File', as shown here.

To install an extra printer press the **Add** button in the 'Printers' dialogue box, choose a printer from the list displayed, and select **Install**. Each time you choose to install a different printer, Windows will ask you to insert a particular disc in the A: drive, so that the appropriate printer driver (a file containing the instructions Windows needs to control that printer) can be copied to your computer's hard disc. Then use the 'Connect' dialogue box to select the print destination, as shown above.

Next, reactivate Word and use the **File, Print Setup** command and highlight the printer you want to use in the 'Select Printer' dialogue box, as shown below.

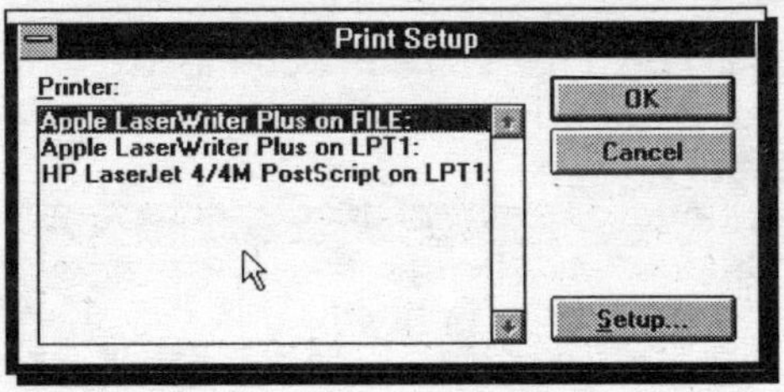

From this dialogue box you can select the default printer or any other installed printer. Next, press **Setup,** select the paper size and orientation needed, and then either press **OK** to confirm your selection, or **Cancel** to abort the procedure.

Now your printer is set up you can, at any time, use the **File, Print** command from the Word menu bar, which opens the 'Print' box, shown on the next page. The settings in this box allow you to select the number of copies, and which pages, you want printed.

The **Options** button gives you access to some more advanced print options, such as printing in reverse order, or with and without annotations, hidden text, field codes or document summary information. The **Setup** option gives you another chance to change your printer settings, before finally selecting **OK**, to send print output from Word to your selection, either the printer connected to your computer, or to an encoded file on disc.

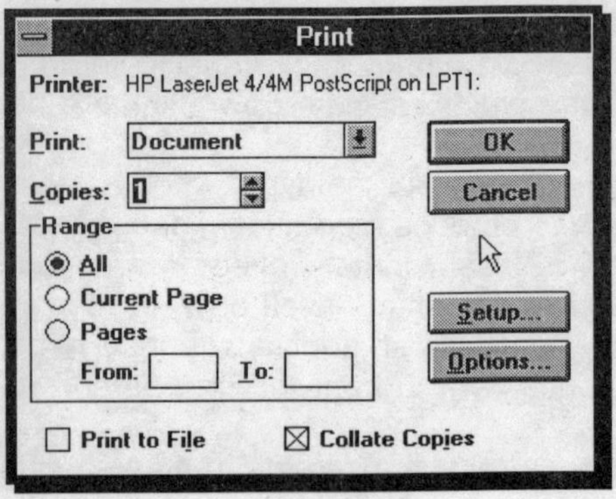

Printing from a File:
An encoded print file, as described above, has all the printer commands embedded in it and can be printed on, for example, a laser printer connected to the first parallel port, by using the simple DOS command

COPY *Filename*/B LPT1

to copy the file to the printer, from the computer connected to it. Word, or indeed Windows, do not need to be running, or even installed, on this computer at all.

Do remember that, whenever you change printers, the appearance of your document may change, as Word uses the fonts available with the newly selected printer. This can affect the line lengths, which in turn will affect both tabulation and pagination of your document.

6. PAGE LAYOUT IN WORD

Page layout is a combination of page format and the paragraph styles and formats of the text and graphics on that page.

Page Format in Word

You can format a page in Word by using the **Format** command from the menu bar, then selecting in turn the various options displayed in the pull-down sub-menu, shown here, from **Paragraph** to **Section Layout**.

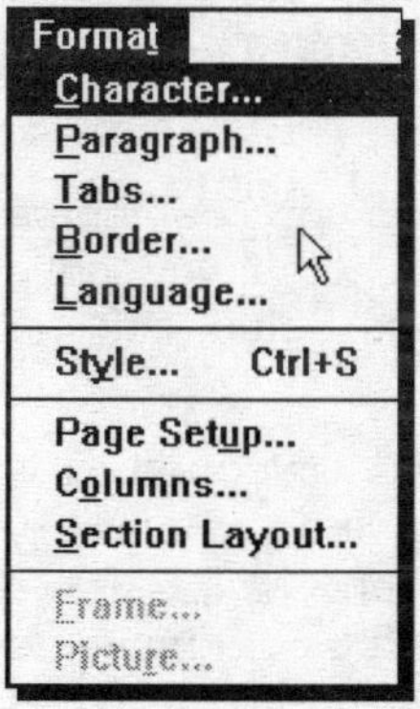

The standard page layout can be set by selecting the **Page Setup** sub-menu. The settings specified therein, can be applied to the whole document, selected text, or from the current cursor position for the rest of the document. Page layout can also be included in the template that you select when you create a document, with the **File**, **New** command, since it includes paragraph styles which in turn specify page settings. A page layout includes settings for the following:

- Left, centre, right, decimal, and leader tab stops
- Top, bottom, left, right, and gutter margins
- Page size and orientation
- Number of columns, and space between each column
- Placement of headers and/or footers
- Section layout commands which control the starting point for the section text, line numbering, vertical alignment of text, and display of footnotes
- Placement and style of lines around page and between columns.

Formatting a Page Setup

You can modify your page set-up from any Word view. However, you can only see the changes you make take effect correctly, if you are in Page Layout mode, or you select the **File, Print Preview** command.

To understand page set-ups you must understand the 'Page Setup' boxes shown in this and subsequent pages. **Open** the PCUSERS3 document, and then open the dialogue box below with the **Format, Page Setup** command. At the top of the dialogue box are three buttons which select the type of page attribute you would like to change.

When the page set-up is altered, Word reformats the document using that set-up. Any changes you make are effective only for the current document, unless you save the page set-up to the existing (or a new) style, or template.

Modifying Margins:

You can change the standard page margins for your entire document, from the cursor position onward, or if you have selected some text prior to opening the 'Page Setup' box, for the selected text.

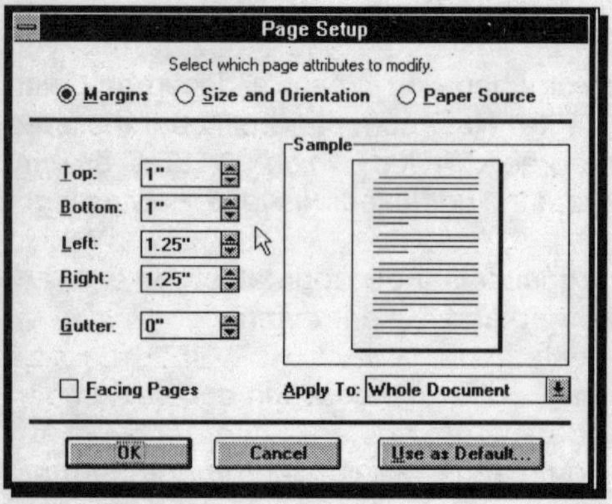

This dialogue box is obtained initially when the **Page Setup** command is selected, or when the 'Margins' option button is clicked. It lets you control your paper margins (the blank areas around the edges).

The 'Sample' page in the middle-right of the box shows, how your changes will look on a real page.

Modifying Paper Size:

Selecting the next option button, 'Size and Orientation', in the above dialogue box, allows you to select the paper size relevant to your printer. In our case, the displayed paper size is A4 (see the screen dump on the next page), since we changed it earlier. Clicking on the down-arrow of the paper size box reveals the available paper and envelope sizes.

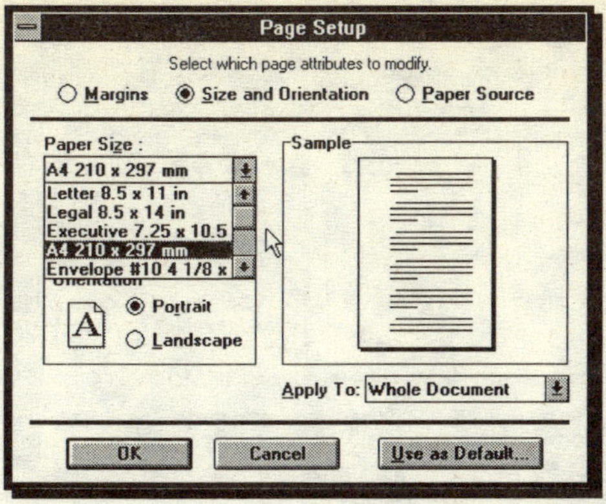

Check that the paper size matches that in your printer, otherwise you may get strange results. The orientation of the printed page is normally **Portrait** (text prints across the page width), but you could choose to change this to **Landscape** which prints across the page length, as long as your printer can print in landscape.

Modifying Paper Source:
Clicking on the third 'Page Setup' button, displays the following:

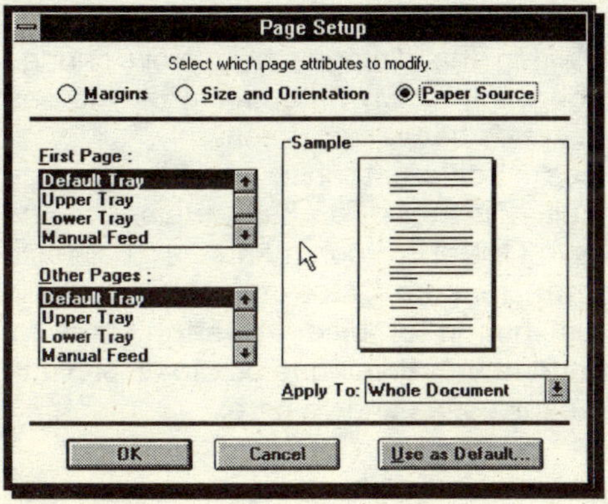

From here you can select the paper source. You might have a printer that holds paper in trays, in which case you might want to specify that the first page (headed paper perhaps), should be taken from one tray, while the rest of the paper should be taken from a different tray.

Formatting Page Columns

You can modify the number displayed columns, either for the whole document or selected text. In the screen overleaf, we have selected the second paragraph of the PCUSERS3 memo and then used the **Format, Columns** command to format it in two columns with 0.5" in between the two columns.

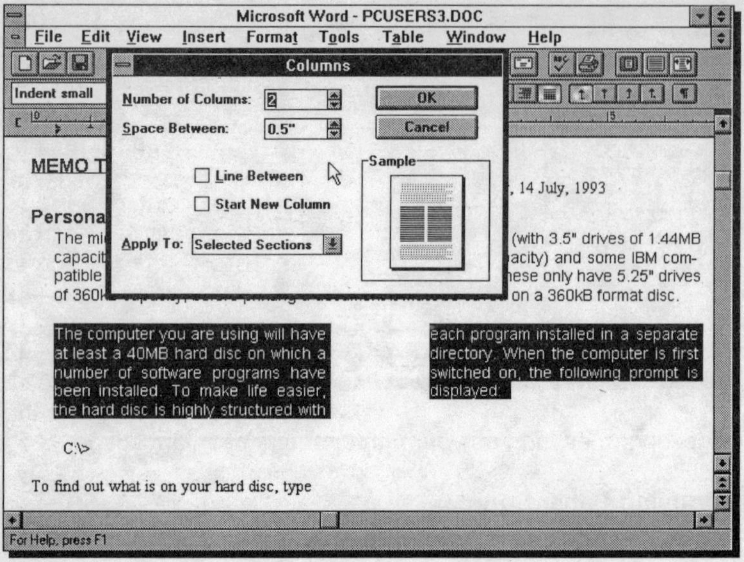

Click on the **Number of Columns** arrows to see how the 'sample' page changes within the dialogue box. Now change the **Space Between** (otherwise known as gutter width) to see how to set the separation zones between columns.

In WORD you can use 4 different units for setting page measurements; the default is inches. To change this, use the **Tools, Options** command and select 'General' from the **Category** list. Click at the 'inches' button of **Measurement Units** at the bottom of the dialogue box to display the other choices, as shown here.

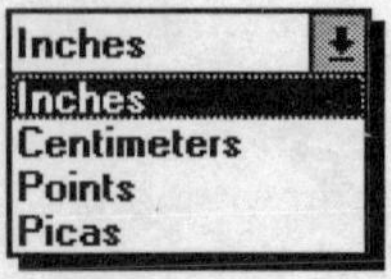

Formatting Page Tabs

You can format text in columns by using tabs. Word has default left tab stops every 0.5 inch from the left margin, which appear as inverted Ts under the ruler's scale (see next page). The default ruler is 8.3 inches long, but this will obviously change depending on the width of page you have specified.

To set tabs, use either the **Format, Tabs** command which produces the Tab dialogue box, or the tab buttons (upward pointing arrows) on the right-hand side of the Ribbon.

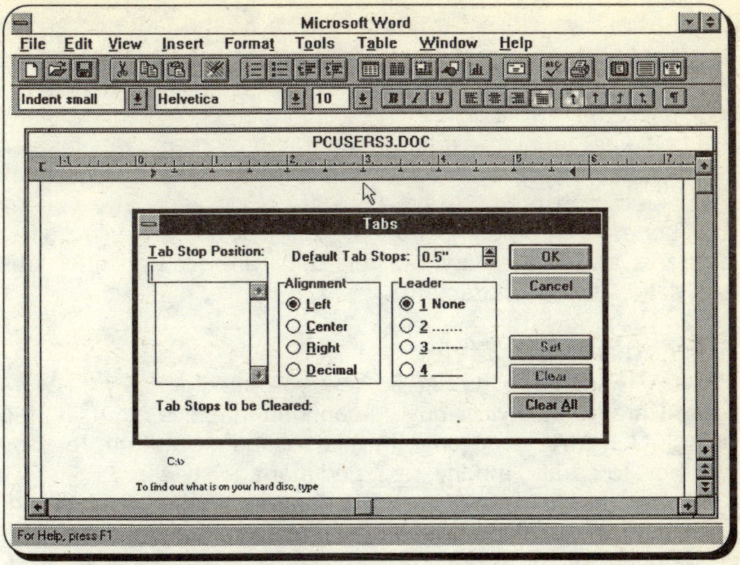

The tab stop types available have the following function:

Button	***Name***	***Effect***
	**Left**	Left aligns text after the tab stop.
	**Centre**	Centres text on tab stop.
	**Right**	Right aligns text after the tab stop.
	**Decimal**	Aligns decimal point with tab stop.

To clear the ruler of tab settings press the **Clear All** button in the Tabs dialogue box. When you set a tab stop on the ruler, all default tab stops to the left of the one you are setting are removed. In addition, tab stops apply either to the paragraph containing the cursor, or to any selected paragraphs.

As all paragraph formatting, such as tab stops, is placed at the end of a paragraph, if you want to carry the formatting of the current paragraph to the next, press <Enter>. If you don't want formatting to carry on, press the down arrow key instead.

The easiest way to set a tab is to click on the tab type button you want and then point and click at the required position on the lower half of the ruler. If you want to remove an added tab, point to it, click and drag it off the ruler.

If you want tabular text to be separated by characters instead of by spaces, click the Leader button in the Tab dialogue box and select one of the three available characters. The options are none (the default), dotted, dashed, or underline. The Contents and Index pages of this book are set with right tabs and dotted leader characters.

Formatting with Styles

We saw earlier in Chapter 5, how you can format your work using Paragraph Styles, but we confined ourselves to using the default NORMAL style only. In this section we will get to grips with how to create, modify, use, and manage styles.

As mentioned previously, a Paragraph Style is a set of formatting instructions which you save so that you can use repeatedly within a document or in different documents. A collection of Paragraph Styles forms a Style Sheet which could be deemed appropriate for, say, all your memos, so it can be used to preserve uniformity. It maintains consistency and saves time by not having to format each paragraph individually. Further, should you decide to change a style, all the paragraphs associated with that style reformat automatically. Finally, if you want to provide a pattern for shaping a final document, then you use what is known as a Template. All documents which have not been assigned a document template, use the NORMAL.DOT template, by default.

Paragraph Styles:

Paragraph Styles contain paragraph and character formats and a name can be attached to these formatting instructions. From then on, applying the style name is the same as formatting that paragraph with the same instructions.

You can create a style by example, either with the use of the Ribbon or the keyboard, or you can create a style from scratch, before you use it, by selecting the **Format, Style** menu command. By far the simplest way of creating a style is by example with the use of the Ribbon.

Creating Paragraph Styles by Example:

In a previous chapter we spent some time manually creating some hanging indents in the last few paragraphs of the PCUSERS3 document. To create a style from this previous work, place the insertion pointer in one of these paragraphs, say, in the 'Name Description' line, and highlight the entire name of the existing style in the Ribbon's Style box, as follows:

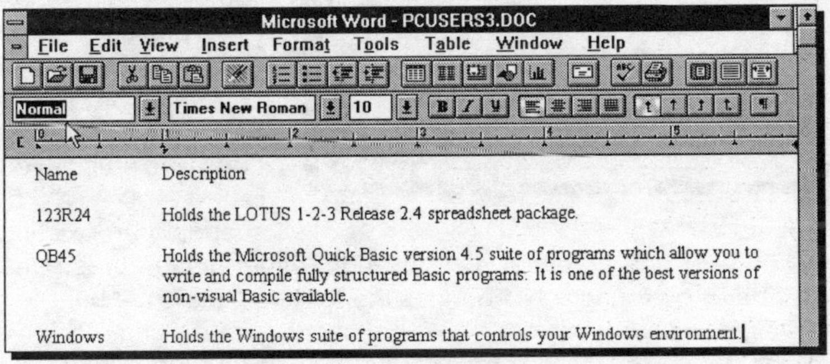

Then, type the new style name you want to create, say, 'Hanging Indent', and press <Enter>.

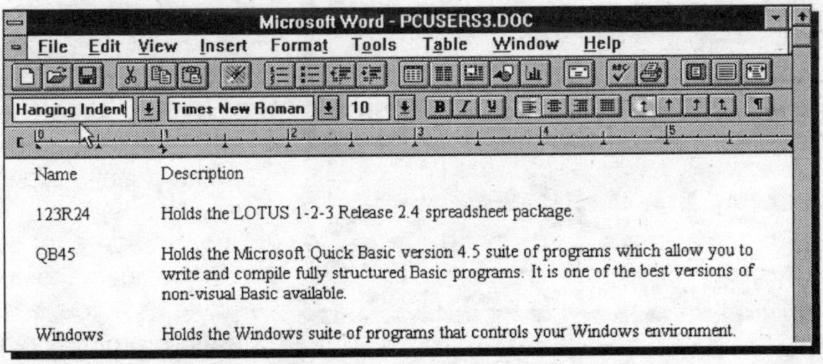

Finally, highlight the last three paragraphs with hanging indents and change their style to the new 'Hanging Indent', by clicking the mouse in the Style box button and selecting the appropriate style from the displayed list.

To do the same thing with the keyboard, place the cursor in the required paragraph, press <Ctrl+S>, and type the new style name. Then, apply the new style as discussed above.

Creating Styles with the Menu Command:
You can create, or change, a style before you apply any formatting to a paragraph, by using the **Format**, **Style** command, which displays the following dialogue box:

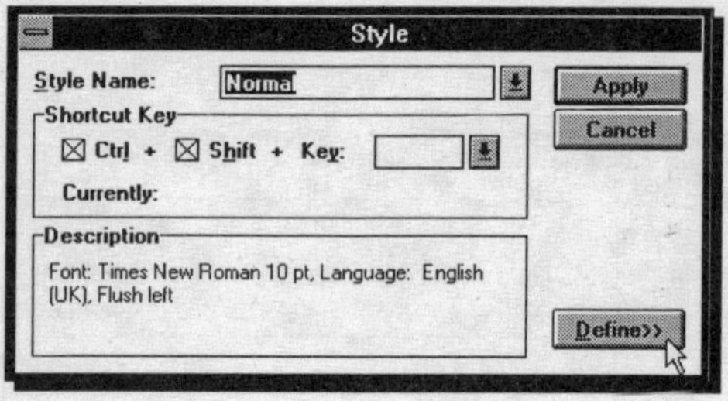

From here you can select which style you want to change by pressing the down arrow button of the **Style Name** box and choosing from the displayed list. If you are not changing an existing style, skip the above procedure. In either case, press the **Define>>** button which produces the following dialogue box:

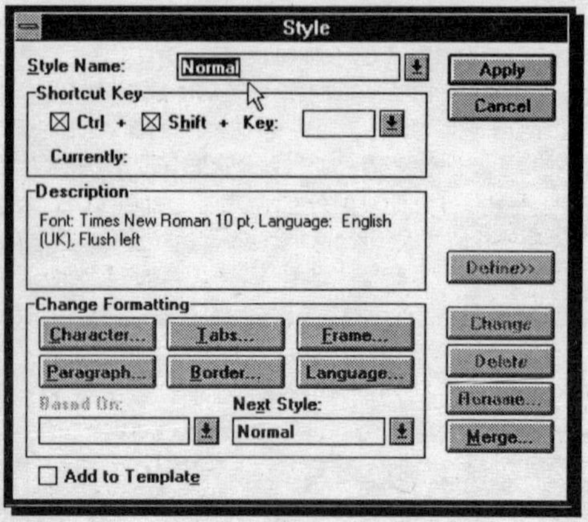

From here you can create a new style, or modify an existing style, by changing the formatting of characters, borders, paragraphs, and tab stops. You can even select which style should follow your current style.

If you have a lot of changes to make to a style, or you are creating your own personal style sheet, then it might be better if you created a template and defined your styles within it. From then on, each time you want to use your special styles, simply begin with your customised template rather than the default NORMAL template.

Note that Word has a default NORMAL template which contains a default NORMAL style sheet with a default Normal paragraph style in it!

Document Templates:
A document template provides the overall pattern of your final document. It can contain:

- Paragraph styles and style sheets, which can control your paragraph and page set-up.
- Boilerplate text, which is text that remains the same in every document.
- Glossary items, which is standard text and graphics that you could insert in a document by typing the name of the glossary entry.
- Macros, which are programs that can change the menus and key assignments to comply with the type of document you are creating.

As we have said before, every document has a template. If you don't assign a template to a document, then the default NORMAL.DOT template is used by Word. To create a new document template, you either modify an existing one, create one from scratch, or create one based on the formatting of an existing document.

To illustrate this last point, we will create a simple document template, which we will call PCUSER, based on the formatting of the PCUSERS3 document. But first, make sure you have defined the 'Hanging Indent' style as explained earlier. Then, select the **File, New** command which displays the New dialogue box, as shown here. From this dialogue box you can create a new document or a new template. Select **New Template**, type in the **Use Template** box the name of the document (and its extension) on which you want the new template to be based, and press **OK**. Next, choose the **File Save As** command, type the template name (PCUSER in this case), fill in the summary information, and press the **OK** button.

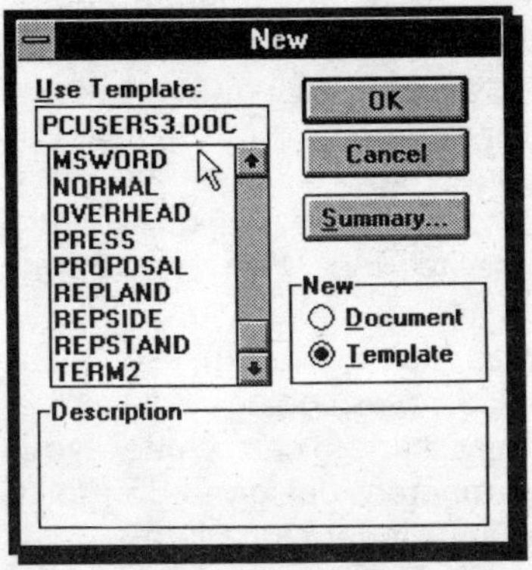

To use the new template, use the **File**, **New** command, which causes the New Dialogue box to be displayed, as shown here. Select the name of the Template you want to use, from the **Use Template** list, and press the **OK** button.

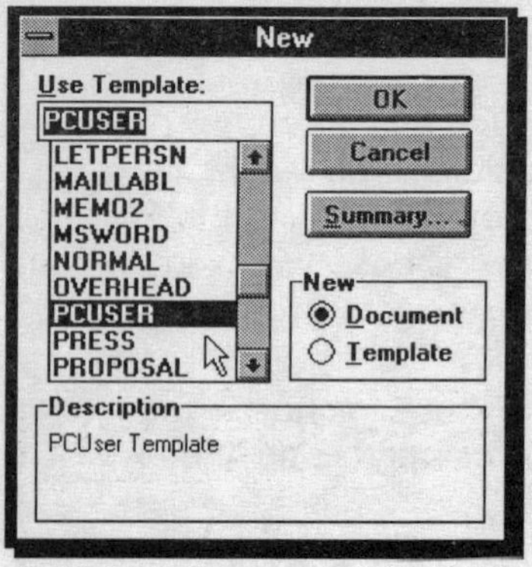

Templates can also contain Macros as well as Glossaries; macros allow you to automate Word keystroke actions only, while glossaries allow you to insert text and graphics from the glossary to your document. Macros and glossaries will be discussed in more detail later in a separate chapter.

To specify the location of a macro or glossary entry into your document, use the **File, Template** command, which displays the Template dialogue box, shown alongside.

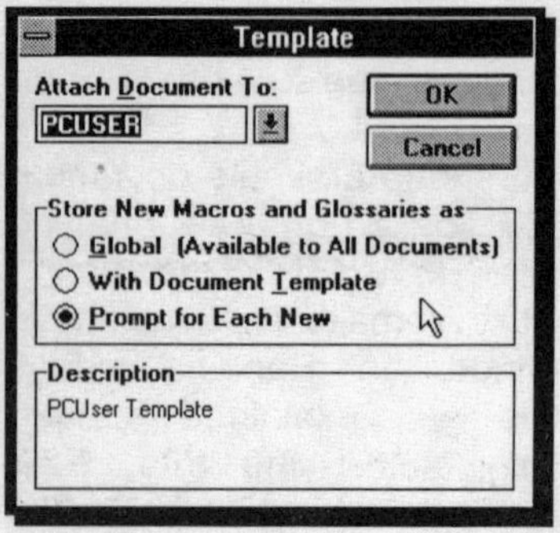

To make the macro and/or glossary entry available to all documents, select the **Global** option button. To make the macro and/or glossary entry only available to documents based on the current template, select the **With Document Template** option button.

Storing macros and/or glossaries as global, makes them available to all your documents. However, doing this with a large number of macros and/or glossaries can clutter your NORMAL.DOT file. That is why macros designed to do a specific job should be kept with the appropriate template.

Special Formatting Features

Word has several special formatting features which force text to override style and style sheet formatting. In what follows, we discuss the most important amongst these.

Changing the Default Character Format:
As we have seen, Word uses the Times Roman type font with a 10 points size as the default for the Normal style, which is contained in the NORMAL template, for all new documents. If the majority of your work demands some different font style or size, then you can change these defaults to suit you.

To change the default character formatting, use the **Format, Character** command, select the new defaults you want to use, and select the **Use as Default** button, as shown below:

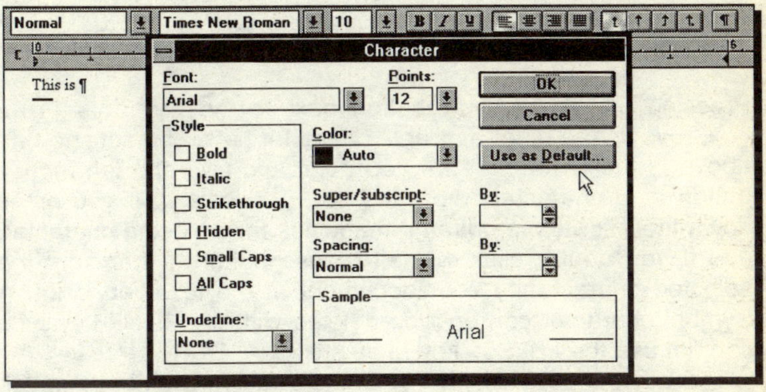

On pressing the **Use as Default** button, the following dialogue box is displayed:

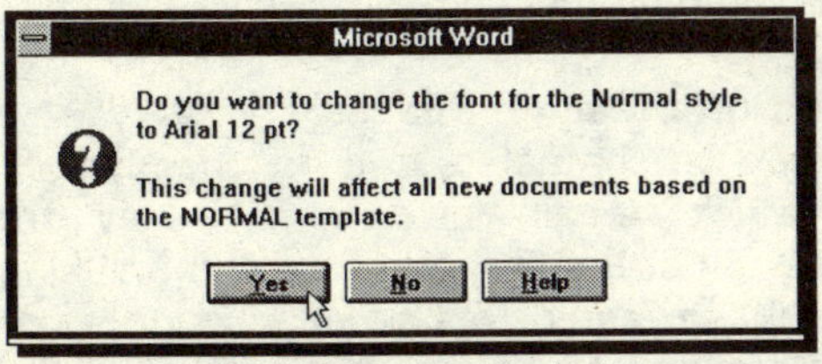

Pressing the **Yes** button changes the default character settings for this and all subsequent new documents, but does not change already existing ones.

Inserting Special Characters and Symbols:
Word has a collection of Symbol fonts, such as the characters produced by the Symbol, Wingdings and Zapf Dingbats character sets, from which you can select characters and insert them into your document using the **Insert, Symbol** command.

On executing this command, Word displays the following dialogue box:

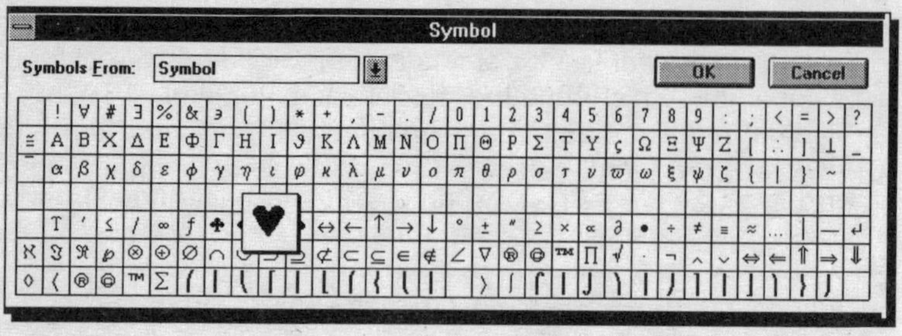

Pressing the down-arrow button next to the **Symbols From** box, reveals the other available character sets. The set showing above is the Symbol set. If you point and click the left mouse button at a character within the set, it selects it. If you press down the left mouse button it magnifies the selected character, and if you double-click the left mouse button, it transfers the selected character to your document at the insertion point. A Symbol character can only be deleted with the <Del> key; you can not use the <BkSp> key to delete it.

The advantage of using Symbol is that Word embeds codes in your document which prevent you from changing the character by selecting it and changing to a different font. Thus, this type of formatting overrides any changes you might introduce with a new paragraph formatting.

Inserting Hyphens and Non-breaking Spaces:
You can include other special characters in a document, such as optional hyphens, which remain invisible until they are needed to hyphenate a word at the end of a line; non-breaking hyphens, which prevent unwanted hyphenation; and non-breaking spaces, which prevent two words from splitting at the end of a line. To insert these characters, use the following key combinations:

Optional hyphen	<Ctrl+–>
Non-breaking hyphen	<Shift+Ctrl+–>
Non-breaking space	<Shift+Ctrl+Spacebar>.

7. FRAMES AND DRAWINGS

A frame in Word is like a 'mini-document' within the main document that allows you to create multiple layouts on the same page. A frame can contain text, a drawing, a picture, or an object such as a Lotus 1-2-3 worksheet, an AmiPro document, or a Word equation. A frame is not affected by the formatting of the main document. You can make document text wrap around, or flow above and below a frame; using the latter, you can create a heading to span a multi-column page. A page can contain multiple frames, but they can not overlap.

Creating Frames

With Word you have the option of creating an empty frame by

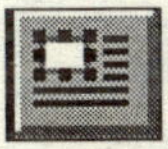

pressing the Frame button on the Toolbar, shown here, or by using the **Insert, Frame** command. You must, however, make sure that you are in Page Layout mode first.

Using either method opens a crosshair on your display and by moving this to the desired position, then clicking and dragging the mouse, you can insert a frame of the required size in your document, as shown below:

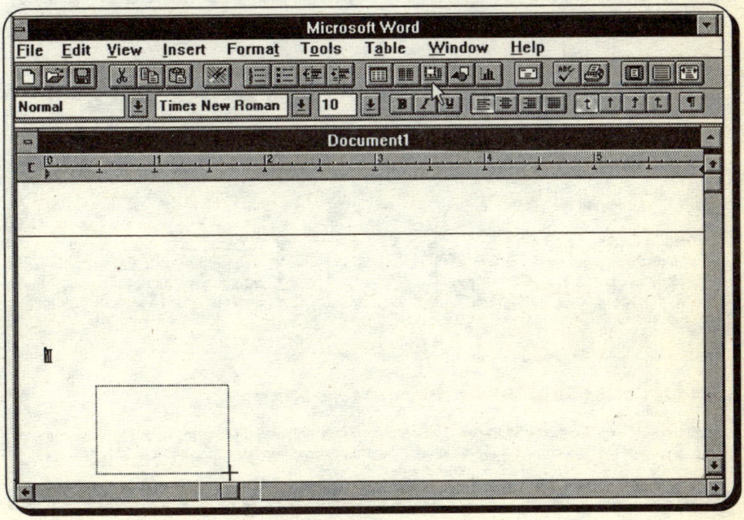

When you create a frame, it is placed in your document with the insertion point blinking in the upper left corner. When you type text within the frame, it wraps to fit the frame, but the frame expands vertically to enable all the typed text to be displayed.

Moving Frames

A frame can be moved around your document by first selecting it, then either dragging it with the mouse (move the mouse pointer over the frame until it turns to a four-headed arrow, then click and drag to the desired position), or by using the **Format, Frame** command, and specifying its exact position on the page in the Frame box.

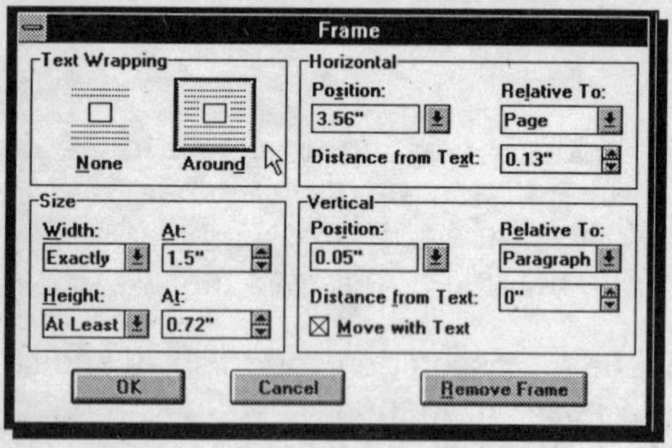

If a frame is placed in the middle of an existing paragraph, the text of that paragraph can either wrap around the frame, as shown below, or it splits above and below the frame. This depends on the selected **Text Wrapping** option in the Frame dialogue box, with **Around** being the default.

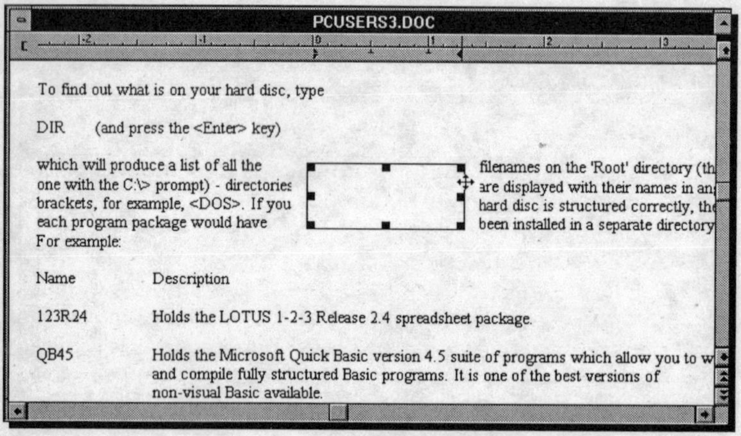

Also by default, framed objects move with their surrounding text. To fix a frame at a specific position on a page, use the **Format, Frame** command and deselect the **Move with Text** option.

Word allows you to select a paragraph, a table or a drawing and then frame it, as shown below:

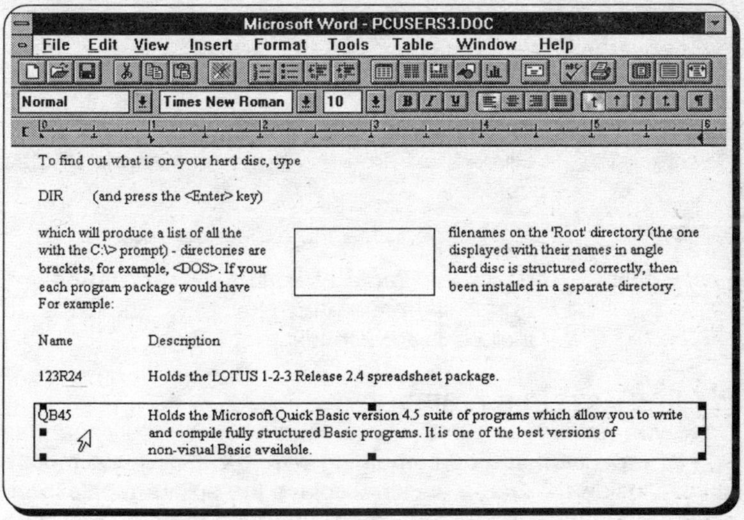

Once an object is framed, it can be moved in exactly the same way as an empty frame. You in fact drag a dotted frame with the pointer, until you release the mouse button, which then fixes the new frame position.

Sizing Frames

There are two ways of sizing frames; with the mouse or the keyboard using the Frame dialogue box.

Sizing a Frame with the Mouse:

To size a frame with the mouse, select it so that the black selection handles appear around the frame, then move the mouse pointer over one of the selection handles until it turns to the two-headed arrow, sizing, arrow. Drag the sizing arrow to change the frame to the required size, then release the mouse button.

Dragging one of the corner handles will drag the two attached frame sides with the pointer, but dragging a centre line handle will only move that side. Try these actions until you are happy with the resultant frame.

Sizing a Frame with the Keyboard:
To size a frame with the keyboard, first select the frame, then use the **Format, Frame** command which displays the Frame dialogue box. In this box, select the Width and Height options.

The available Width and Height options have the following functions:

Auto	Gives the frame the same size as the framed object.
Exactly	Makes the frame the exact size you specify.
At Least	Gives the frame at least the specified height, but it increases the height to be able to include the whole text, or graphic.

Placing Text in a Frame

Once you have your frame where you want it on the page, it is only of any use if you do something with it. So, click the mouse pointer inside the frame, which displays the sizing handles and places the cursor inside the frame, and type in some text (see screen display on next page). In our example, we also chose to name the style within the frame as 'framed'.

Next, and while the cursor is within the frame, select 'hanging indent' as the new style for the text inside your frame. The frame disappears, but the text remains as a redefined paragraph. If you choose the 'framed' style, the frame will reappear with the text intact inside it.

Now save this as PCUSERS4, then click the mouse button outside the frame. This will cancel the frame selection and you will not be able to access, or edit, the text inside the frame until you next click inside it. Moving the mouse pointer over the frame area, turns it into a four-headed arrow, allowing you to move the frame to a new position when you click and drag. You can select the frame by single clicking which will let you resize it; clicking once more anywhere on the text within the frame, allows you to edit that text.

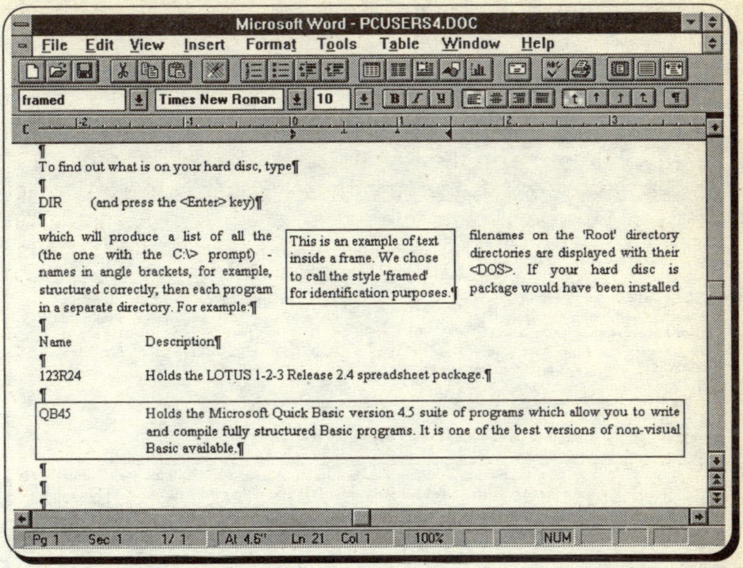

Importing a Picture into a Frame

Create another frame on your page and click inside to select it. To import a picture into this frame, select the **Insert, Picture** command, which will open the dialogue box shown below.

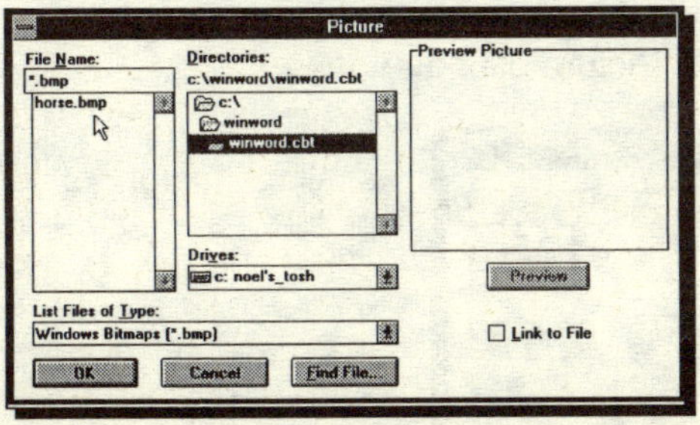

This box allows you to enter the details of the picture, or graphic, that you want to import. The **List Files of Type** box gives you the choice of a wide range of graphic formats to import, but we will stick to a Word graphics sample, to be found in the **winword.cbt** subdirectory. This file is called **horse.bmp** and is a Windows bitmap file. First, change the **List Files of Type** box to Windows bitmap, which will list all the **.bmp** files, then select the file from the correct subdirectory, and press the **OK** button.

Word inserts the picture in the selected frame, as shown below:

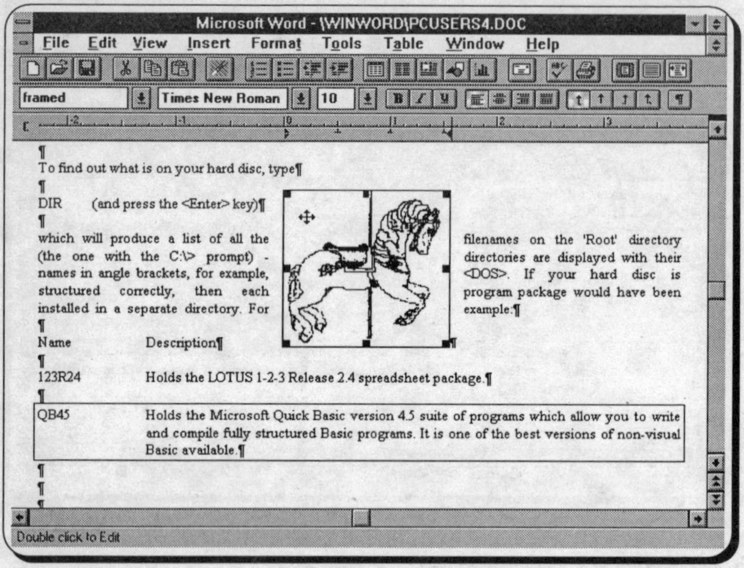

Save the resultant document as PCUSERS5. There is a wealth of clip-art files in the **clipart** subdirectory, but to access them you must first change the **List Files of Type** box to Windows Metafile, which displays the **.wmf** files. You can preview each selected file (before inserting it into your document, by pressing the **Preview** button in the Picture dialogue box.

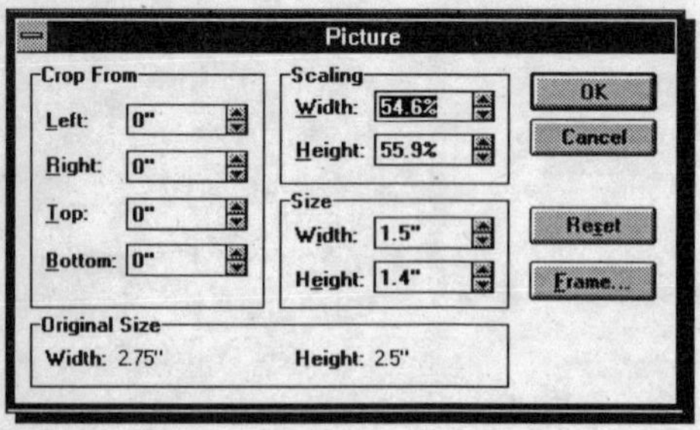

You can change the scaling factor of a picture and size it either by using the mouse, or by using the **Format**, **Picture** command. The latter method causes the Picture dialogue box to be displayed, as shown here.

If you want more white space around a picture, use negative numbers in the **Crop From** fields.

A picture can be inserted directly into your document at the cursor position, or you can first insert a frame, then insert the picture into the frame. The advantage of the latter is that your text can be made to wrap around a frame, so you have more control over the inserted picture.

You can add a variety of borders to a frame, or a picture, by using the **Format**, **Border** command which displays the following dialogue box:

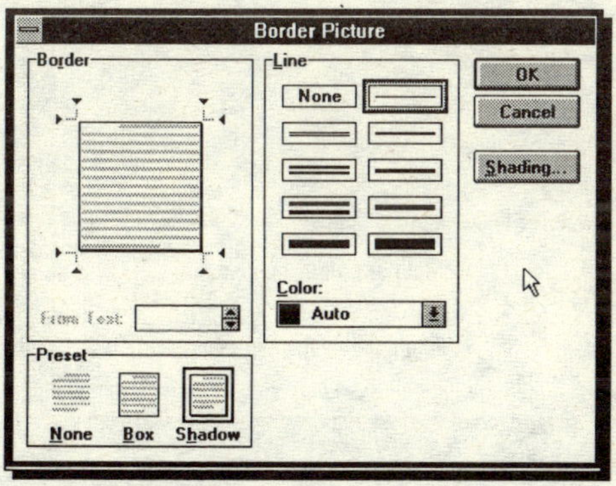

From here, you can select the thickness of the border line, whether it will have a single-line border, or a double-line border, and whether the border should have a shadow or not. You can also choose the type of shading you prefer within the border area, by pressing the **Shading** button.

The Drawing Tool

You can edit any picture with the use of the Microsoft Draw tool. You can also use it to create, or edit, a drawing consisting of lines, arcs, ellipses, and rectangles; these can either exist in their own right, or be additions to a picture. You cannot, though, create a drawing in a frame that already contains text. This can be seen by selecting a frame then using the **Edit** command which displays the pull-down sub-menu. You can only use the Drawing tool if the last entry of that sub-menu has changed to the one shown here.

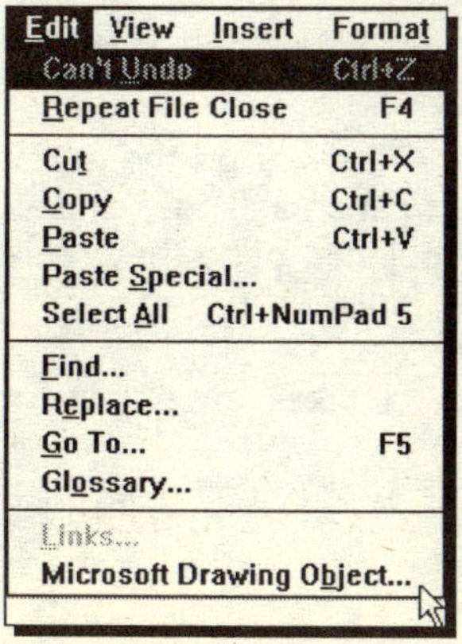

The Draw tool can be activated by either using the **Microsoft Drawing Object** option from the **Edit** menu, or by double-clicking within a picture.

Microsoft Draw is an OLE (object linking and embedding) type of program which is included with Word for Windows. As mentioned over the page, you can activate the Draw tool with a

preselected picture or drawing, or you can press the Draw button on the Toolbar, shown here, which causes the following screen to be displayed.

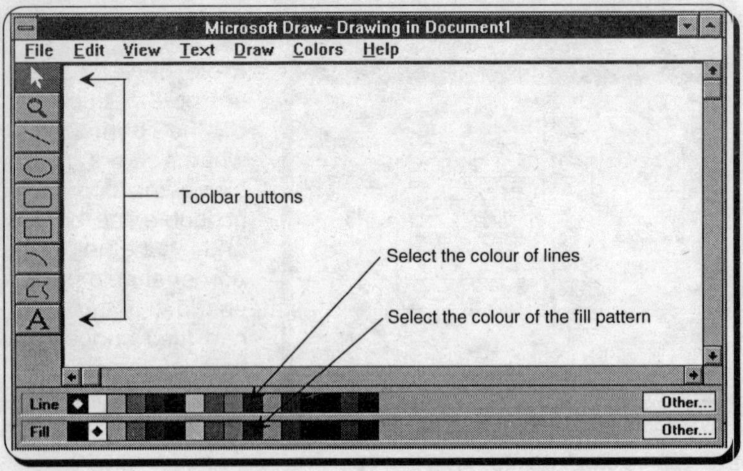

Using the Microsoft Draw tool, you create and select objects in a picture, then copy and move them, or change their size and shape, etc. These options can be carried out either by using the Toolbar on the left of the Draw screen or by using the Draw pull-down menus.

Using the Draw Toolbar:
Word provides a variety of buttons in the Toolbar on the left of the Draw screen, both for creating objects such as lines, circles, or squares and for manipulating these objects, once they have been selected. The buttons on the Draw toolbar are:

Selection Arrow - Selects or sizes an object, or group of objects.

Magnifying Glass - Selects a specified area of a picture and magnifies it.

Line - Draws a straight line in the direction you drag the mouse. To draw a line at a perfect 45 degree angle, hold <Shift> while dragging the mouse.

Ellipse - Draws an ellipse. To draw a circle, hold <Shift> while dragging the mouse.

Rounded Rectangle - Draws a rectangle with rounded corners. To draw a rounded square, hold <Shift> and drag the mouse.

Rectangle - Draws a rectangle. To draw a square, hold <Shift> and drag the mouse.

Arc - Draws an arc. You can create a Bezier curve by modifying an arc.

Freehand/Polygon - Draws freehand lines, or draws polygons. When you finish, press <Esc>.

Text - Places the insertion point inside a drawing so you can type text, each paragraph of which will become an object, which you can then manipulate.

Draw Menu Commands:

Most of the menu commands available with Microsoft Draw are self-explanatory. The few that are not, are listed below with details of their function.

Command	***Function***
File, Select All	Selects, or deselects, all the objects inside the frame.
File, Bring to Front	Places the selected object on top of all other objects at that location.
File, Send to Back	Places the selected object underneath all other objects at that location.
Draw, Group	Groups the selected objects inside the frame.
Draw, Ungroup	Ungroups the selected objects inside the frame.
Draw, Filled	Changes the fill pattern of the selected object to the current fill pattern.
Draw, Pattern	Displays colour and fill pattern options.

Draw, Line Style	Displays line styles available and thickness of lines.
Draw, Snap to Grid	Aligns objects automatically, or manually, on the grid specified for the frame.
Draw, Show Guides	Displays guide lines inside the frame.
Draw, Rotate/Flip	Rotates/flips the selected object, or group of objects, clockwise or anticlockwise.

Creating a Drawing:
To create an object, click on the required Draw button, such as the ellipse, position the mouse pointer where you want to create the object on the screen, and then drag the mouse to draw the object. Hold the <Shift> key while you drag the mouse to create a perfect circle, square, or rounded square. If you do not hold <Shift>, Word creates an ellipse, a rectangle, or a rounded rectangle.

You can use the freehand/polygon Draw button to create freehand objects. First click on the Freehand button, then position the mouse pointer where you want to create the object on the screen. If you then press the left mouse button and keep it pressed, the mouse pointer changes to the shape of a pencil with which you can draw freehand. If, on the other hand, you click the left mouse button, the edge of the line attaches itself on the drawing area, at the point of contact, and the pointer changes to a crosshair. A straight line can then be drawn between that point and the next point on which you happen to click the mouse button. In this way you can draw polygons. When you finish drawing with either of these two methods, press the <Esc> key to finish.

Editing a Drawing:
To select an object, first click the 'Selection Arrow' button and then click the desired object. Word displays black handles around the object selected.

You can move an object, or multiple objects, within a drawing by selecting them and dragging to the desired position. To copy an object, click at the object, then use the **Edit, Copy / Edit, Paste** commands.

To size an object within Draw, position the mouse pointer on a black handle and then drag the handle until the object is the desired shape and size. This cannot be done to a text object from within Draw, but it can if it is exported to a Word document. If you size a text object in a Word document, Word changes the point size of the text automatically.

To delete an object from either within Word or Draw, select the object and press <Del>. To delete a drawing from either within Word or Draw, hold the <Shift> key down and click each object in turn that makes up the drawing, then press <Del>. From within Draw you could use instead the **Edit, Select All** command, and then press <Del>.

Do try out some of these commands using the two document files that you saved earlier as PCUSERS4 and PCUSERS5. You can experiment with different text fonts with the first document file, and you can try to edit the horse picture with the second document file. As long as you do not save the results of your experimentation under the same file names, you can try different variations to the layout of these documents without fear of losing the contents of the original files.

Using Layered Drawings:

You can use Draw's **Edit**, **Bring to Front** or **Send to Back** commands to determine the order of layered drawings. Drawings, or pictures, layered on top of each other can create useful visual effects, provided you remember that the top drawing/picture obscures the one below it, as shown here.

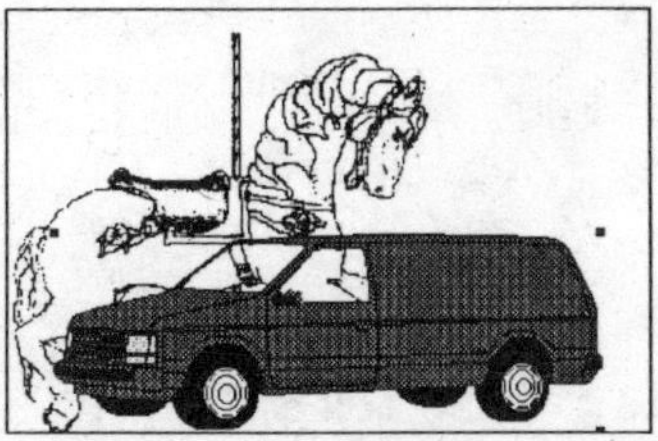

To import the van into Draw, we used Draw's **File, Import Picture**, command, changed directory by double-clicking the [..] entry in the 'Directories' listing, then selected the **clipart** subdirectory and chose the **2doorvan.wmf** file from the 'Files' listing. Note that the van picture is the one in the foreground (it obscures the horse). You can reverse this situation by first selecting the horse (by double-clicking at its image away from the van selection area), then using the **Edit, Bring to Front** command.

Using Line and Fill:

You can use the 'Line' and 'Fill' colour palette at the bottom of Draw's screen, to specify the colour of the lines and the colour of the fill pattern for selected drawings/pictures. The first time you access MS Draw, the line colour is black and the fill pattern is transparent.

Here, we brought the picture of the horse to the foreground, so that it obscures the van, then we selected transparent lines and a coloured fill pattern. Finally, we forced the van to face in the opposite direction, by first selecting it, then using the **Draw, Rotate/Flip** command and selecting the **Flip Horizontal** option. Next, try ungrouping the various drawing sections that make up the van picture, and move them to separate parts of the screen. The effect you get can be quite funny.

Inserting Objects into a Document

You can insert an Object into a document by using the **Insert, Object** command which causes the following dialogue box to appear on your screen:

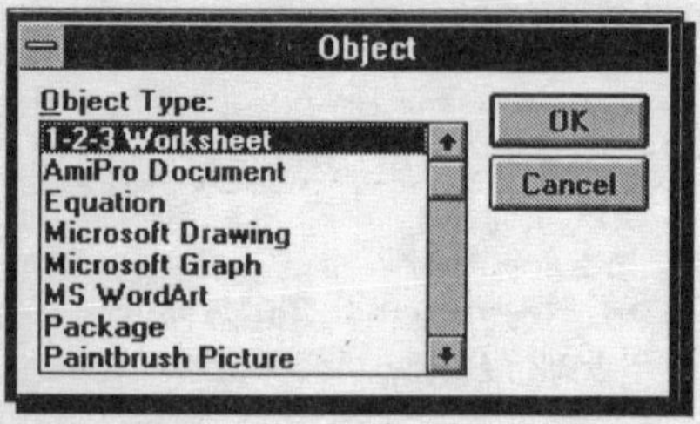

From here, you can choose different 'Object Types', from Lotus 1-2-3 Worksheets to Word Documents. For example, if you select 'Equation' from the **Object Type** list, Word displays the equation editor shown on the next page. This allows you to build mathematical equations which can then be included in your Word for Windows document.

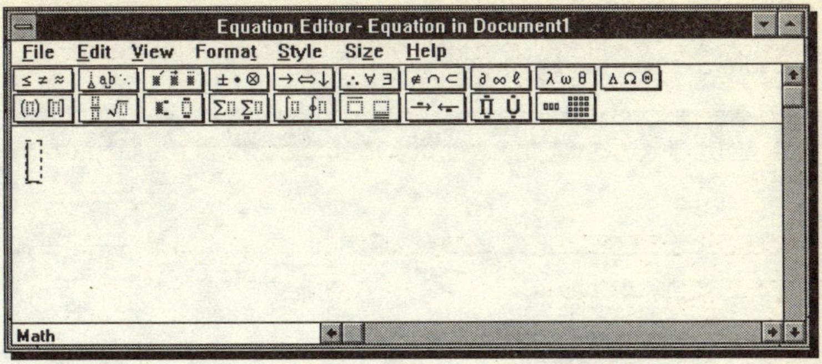

If, on the other hand, you select Microsoft Graph, or you press

the Graph button on Word's Toolbar, shown here, and you don't have a table in your document, the following screen is displayed:

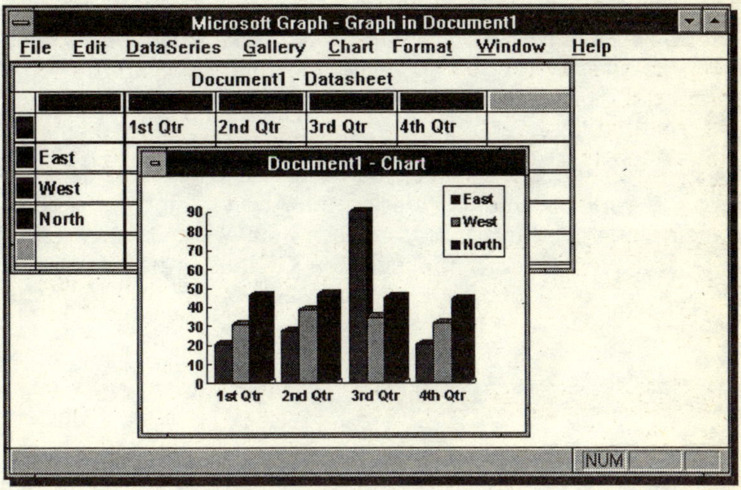

This is an internal Word example, showing the capabilities of the package. If you did have a table within your document which included information that could be graphed (see next chapter), and you had selected the area of the table you wanted to display as a graph, then Word would have displayed the contents of the selected portion of your table in an appropriate chart-type graph.

Finally, selecting MS WordArt, causes the following dialogue box to appear on your screen:

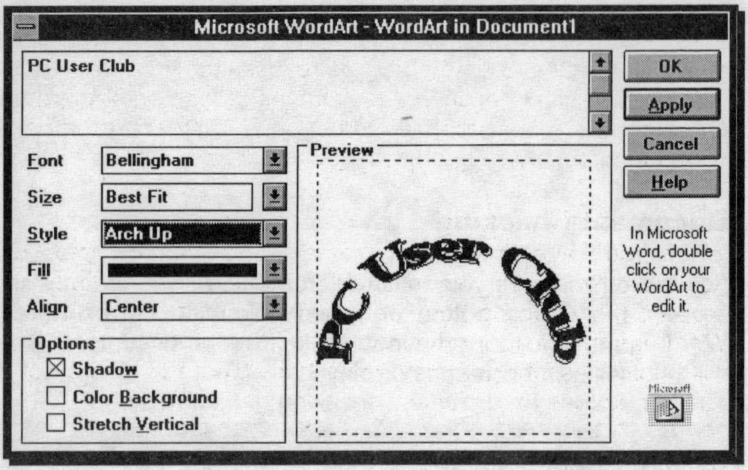

We have typed in the text area 'PC User Club', then selected the 'Arch Up' Style. You can choose from a selection of different fonts, size, and styles which can then be aligned in different areas of your document. Pressing the **Apply** button causes the transfer of you artwork to the document without leaving the Microsoft WordArt, and pressing the **OK** button transfers your artwork to your document and causes you to exit Microsoft WordArt.

8. MORE ADVANCED TECHNIQUES

Microsoft has built many advanced features into Word. Amongst these, we will examine here what you are most likely going to need and in the order we assume you will require them. We shall examine document spell and grammar checking, the use of the thesaurus, page numbering, inclusion of headers/footers, footnotes, tables and charts.

Document Checking

When you have entered all the text and graphics into your document and selected suitable formats, there is only the process of correcting your work before printing the final copy. Word has many built-in tools to speed this process up and we will briefly describe the main ones here. There is also a set of Toolbar buttons for document checking and correcting.

Using the Spell Checker:

Most people have trouble spelling at least some words, but with Word that is not a problem. The package has a very comprehensive spell checker with two dictionaries. The main dictionary contains more that 100,000 words which cannot be edited. The other is a user dictionary that you can customise and edit. When you use the spell checker and choose **Add**, Word adds the word to the user dictionary, which has the file name Custom.dic.

To spell check your document, either click the 'Spell check' button on the Toolbar, shown here, or use the **Tools**, **Spelling** command to open the dialogue box below. Word starts spell checking from the point of insertion onwards. If you want to check a word or paragraph only, highlight it first. If you want to spell check the whole document, move the insertion point to the beginning of the document before starting.

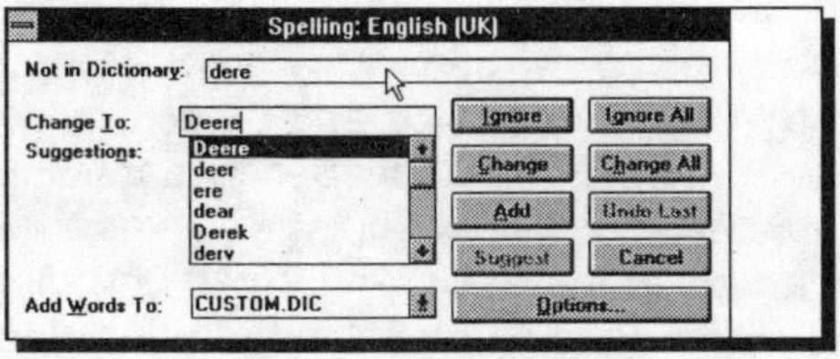

Once Word has found a misspelled word, you can correct it in the **Change To** box, or select a word from the **Suggestions** list. Word will produce a suggestions list only if the **Always Suggest** option from the Options dialogue box, shown here, is checked. This dialogue box is displayed if you press the **Options** button from the opening dialogue box.

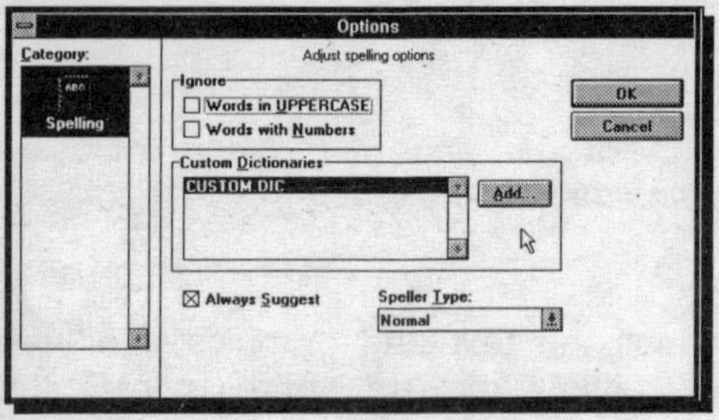

In the Options dialogue box you can select **Words in UPPERCASE** which will cause the spell checker to ignore words in all uppercase letters, and/or you can select **Words with Numbers** which forces the spell checker to ignore all words that include numbers.

When the correct word appears in the **Change To** box (you could choose a different word from the **Suggestions** list), select the **Change** button to replace the misspelled word in your document with the selected word. You select the **Change** button to correct only the current error, otherwise use the **Change All** button to change every future occurrence of incorrect word in the document.

If you don't want to change the word in your document, use the **Ignore** button to leave that word as is, or the **Ignore All** button to ignore all future occurrences of the word in the document. If, on the other hand, Word comes across a specialised word that thinks it is misspelled, but it is not, you can add it to the customised dictionary named in the **Add Words to** box. This customised dictionary is kept in the **WinWord** directory and can be opened like any other file, so that you can edit it. Words are kept in it in alphabetical order.

When Word finds double words, for example, yes yes, the **Not in Dictionary** box changes to the **Repeated Word** box with the repeated word displayed, and the **Change** button becoming a **Delete** button. If you want to delete one of the repeated words, leave the **Change To** box blank, and press the **Delete** button.

Using the Thesaurus:
If you are not sure of the meaning of a word, or you want to use an alternative word to the one you are using currently in your document, then the thesaurus is an indispensable tool. To use the thesaurus, simply place the cursor on the word you want to look up and select **Tools, Thesaurus**. As long as the word is recognised the following box will open.

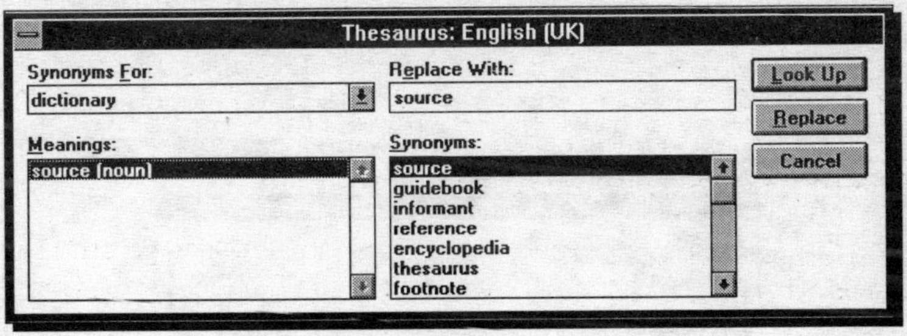

This is a very powerful tool. You can see information about an item in the **Meanings** list, or you can look up a synonym in the **Synonym** list. To change the word in the **Replace With** text box, select an offered word in either the **Meanings** or **Synonyms** list box, or type a word directly into the text box.

You can use the thesaurus like a simple dictionary by typing any word into the **Replace With** box and selecting **Look Up**. If the word is recognised, lists of its meaning variations and synonyms will be displayed. Pressing the **Replace** button will place the word into the document.

The Grammar Checker:
The grammar checker provided with Word, and indeed with other word processors, we feel falls in a different league to the spell checker and the thesaurus. The idea is excellent, but whenever we have tried to use it we have given up in exasperation.

In order to illustrate what happens when using the grammar checker, open the PCUSERS5 file and select the **Tools, Grammar** command. The dialogue box shown on the next page appears on the screen when the last sentence of the paragraph above the dialogue box is being analysed. Note the contents of the **Suggestions** text box.

This same message was also given for every sentence in the document prior to the one being analysed at this point. The message reads 'This main clause may contain a verb in the passive voice'.

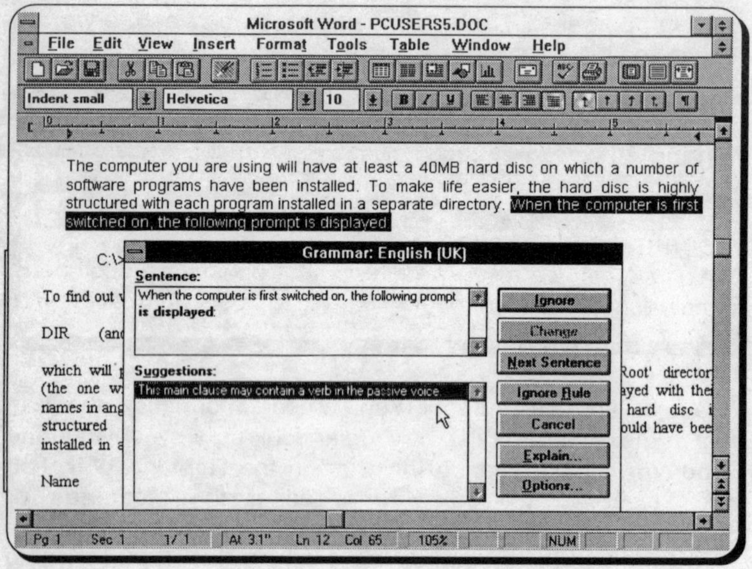

On pressing the **Explain** button, the Grammar Explanation box, shown below, is displayed.

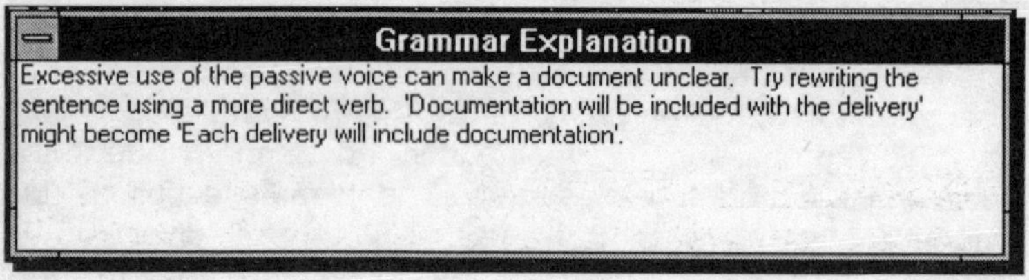

With Word's grammar checker, you have the choice of three types of writing styles, namely Strictly (All Rules), For Business Writing, and For Casual Writing. One of these can be selected by pressing the **Options** button of the Grammar dialogue box, which displays the following:

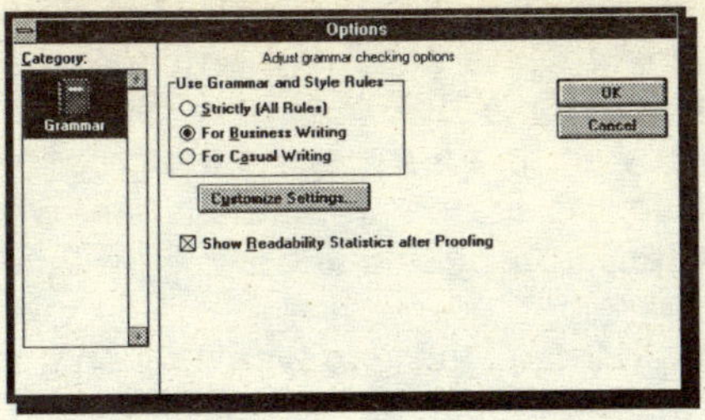

The analysis carried out previously was made with the **For Business Writing** option selected, which perhaps explains the comments of the grammar checker. When the option was changed to **For Casual Writing**, the same suggestions were made regarding the 'passive voice' with the same explanations!

Document Enhancements

In this section we discuss features that enhance a document's appearance, such as page numbering, use of headers and footers, and use of footnotes.

Page Numbering:

If you need to number the pages of a document, but not the first page, use the **Insert, Page Numbers** command, which displays the following dialogue box:

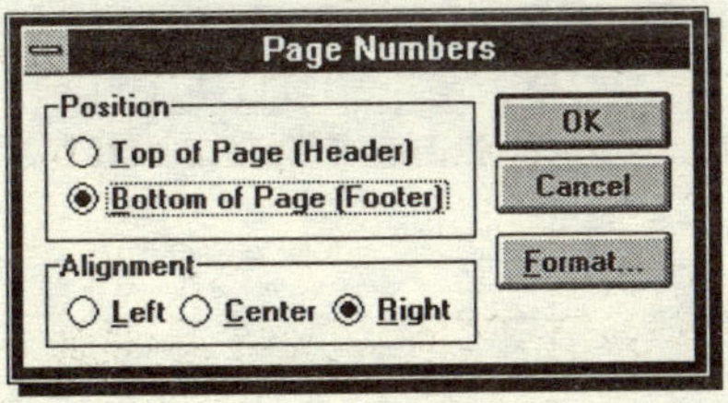

It is in this box you decide where on the page of your document you want the page numbers to appear, and what their alignment should be. Selecting the **Format** button, opens another dialogue box, as shown below:

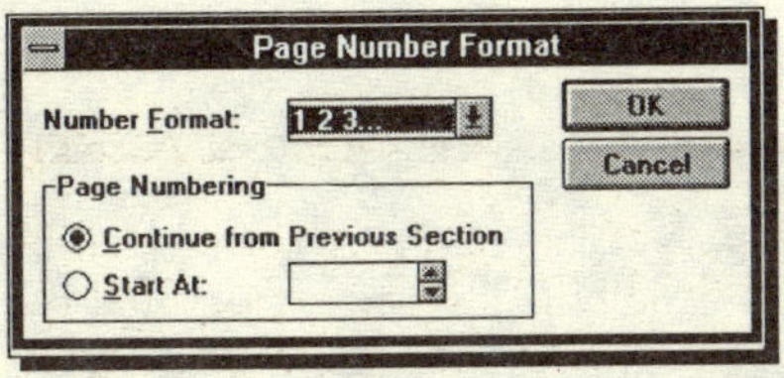

From this dialogue box you can select the **Number Format** from the following alternatives, '1, a, A, i, or I'; the more usual style being the first option, as used in this book. The 'Page Numbering' option gives you two alternatives; **Continue from Previous Section**, or **Start At** a specified number.

To illustrate page numbering with the **Insert, Page Numbers** command, we need a document which is more than one page long. This is because this command only numbers from the second page onwards (if you want the first page numbered, or you need to include leading text to the page numbers, you will have to use the **View, Header/Footer** command, which will be discussed shortly).

To obtain a long document, without having to type it, open the PCUSERS3 file, move the insertion point to the end of the file and use the **Insert, File** command, and select the PCUSERS4 file, then move the insertion point to the end of the combined file and insert the PCUSERS5 file. In this way the three files are joined together forming a document of the required length.

Now move the insertion pointer to the end of the second page so that you can see the page separator line, and use the **Insert, Page Numbers** command, select **Bottom of Page, Centre** and press the **Format** button, select **Start At 1** in the second dialogue box, and press the **OK** button twice. The result is a number '2' appearing centrally in a footer at the bottom of page 2, as shown below.

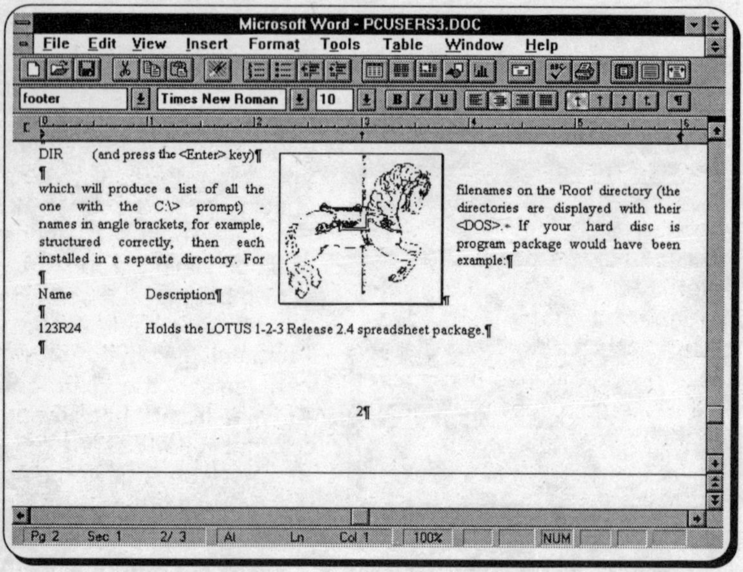

Using Headers and Footers:

Headers consist of text placed in the top margin area of a page, whereas footers are text in the bottom margin. Simple headers or footers in Word can consist of text and a page number, which are produced in the same position of every page in a document, while more complicated ones can also contain graphics images.

Normally, headers and footers are positioned at the top or bottom margins of a page, although Word allows you to position these at any point within a page. In addition, you can have one header/footer for the first page of a document, or section of a document, and a different one for the rest of the document. Word also allows you to select a different header or footer for odd or even pages.

To insert a header or footer in a document, first make sure you are in **Normal** view, then select the **View, Header/Footer** command, which causes Word to display the following dialogue box:

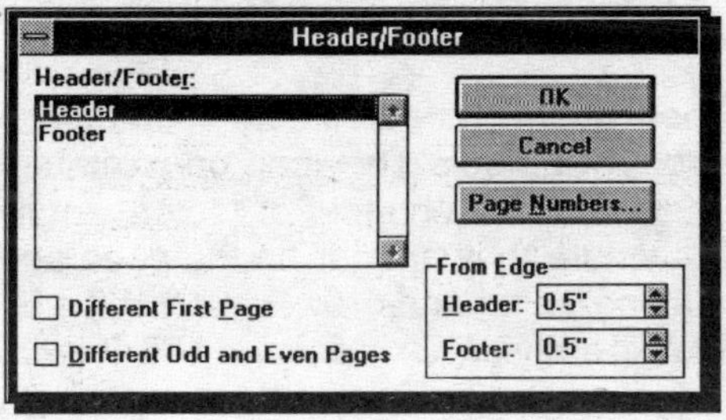

From here you can select Header or Footer, and whether you want a different header or footer on the first page or a different header or footer on odd and even pages by checking either of the two boxes at the bottom of the dialogue box.

To illustrate the point, use the PCUSERS5 document, select **Footer** from the **Header/Footer** list box, press the **Page Numbers** button, and select **Start At** and type 85. On pressing the **OK** button twice, Word displays a pane at the bottom of the page and puts the insertion pointer in it.

In the example shown overleaf, we chose to type in the footer pane the word 'Page', followed by a space, then we pressed the page number button on the pane's ribbon, which inserted the numeral 85, then we pressed <Tab> and typed 'Chapter 8', then pressed <Tab> again, and pressed the time button.

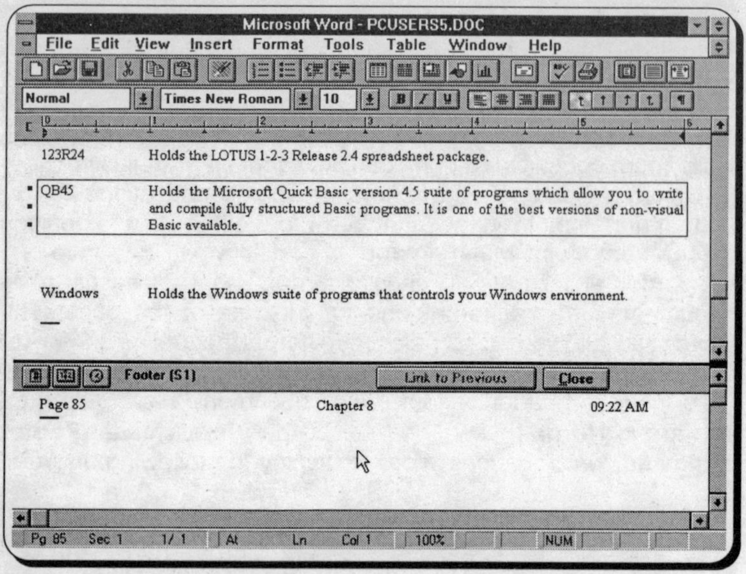

Once you select the **Close** button, headers and footers can only be seen in the **Page Layout** mode. They can be formatted and edited like any other text. To edit a header or footer, simply move the insertion point to where they appear on the page and use the editing and formatting commands, or Ribbon buttons, available to you. Note that the styles for headers and footers are named by Word automatically as 'header' and 'footer'.

A header, or a footer, can be repositioned in several ways. Perhaps the two easiest methods are:

1 If you want to reposition headers or footers within the selected margins of a header or footer, select the **File, Print Preview** command and press the **Margins** button. Dotted lines appear around the header or footer which can then be moved vertically within the available space.

2 If you want to move a header or footer to any position within a page, select it and use the **Insert, Frame** command to put a frame around it. You can then drag the frame to any position on the page.

Using Footnotes:
If your document requires footnotes at the end of each page, or endnotes at the end of each chapter, they are very easy to add and later, if necessary, to edit. Place the cursor at the position you want the reference point to be in the document and select **Insert, Footnote**, which opens the simulated dialogue boxes shown below:

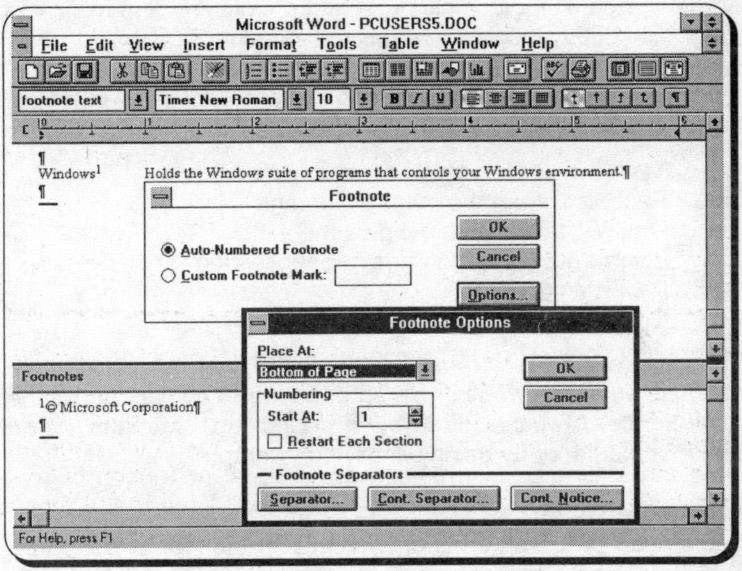

This displays both the two dialogue boxes and the results obtained, on the same screen. The first reference point was placed after the word 'Windows'. The default option in the first dialogue box is **Auto Numbered Footnote**. If you choose to press the **Options** button in this box, Word displays a second dialogue box, as shown above, from which you can select whether you want the footnote at the 'Bottom of the Page', 'Beneath the Text', or at the 'End of the Document'. You could also choose from this second dialogue box the starting number of the reference, and the type of separator.

If you wanted to type a reference mark of your own choosing, then select the **Custom Footnote Mark** from the first dialogue box. You could then use up to ten characters, such as daggers.

Using Tables in Documents

The ability to use 'Tables' is built into most top-range word processors these days. At first glance the process might look complicated and perhaps only a small percentage of users take advantage of the facility, which is a pity because using a 'Table' has many possibilities. If you have worked with a spreadsheet, such as Excel or Lotus 1-2-3, then you are familiar with tables.

Tables are used to create adjacent columns of text and numeric data. A table is simply a grid of columns and rows with the intersection of a column and row forming a rectangular box which is referred to as a 'cell'. In Word you can include pictures, charts, notes, footnotes, tabs, and page breaks in your tables. There are several ways to place information into a table:

- Type the desired text, or numeric data.
- Paste text from the main document.
- Link two tables within a document.
- Insert data created in another application.
- Import a picture.
- Create a chart on information held in a table.

The data is placed into individual cells that are organised into columns and rows, similar to a spreadsheet. You can modify the appearance of table data by applying text formatting and enhancements, or by using different paragraph styles.

Creating a Table:

Tables can be created either by pressing the 'Table' button on the toolbar, shown here, or by using the **Table, Insert Table** command. Using the latter, displays the following dialogue box which enables you to size the column widths at that point.

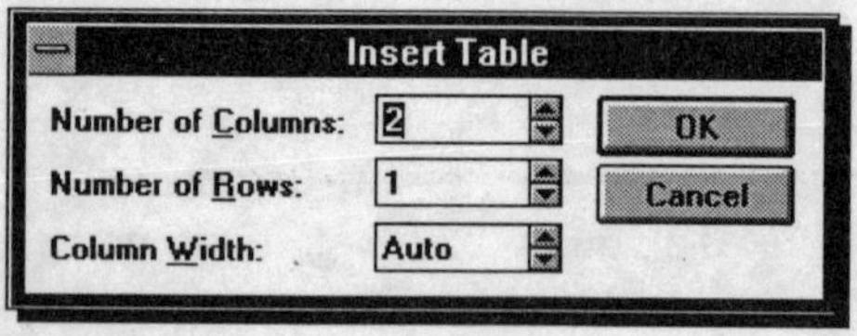

As an example we will step through the process of creating the table shown on the next page. Open the PCUSERS5 file, place the insertion point at the end of the file (or where you want the table), then click on the 'Table' button and drag down and to the right.

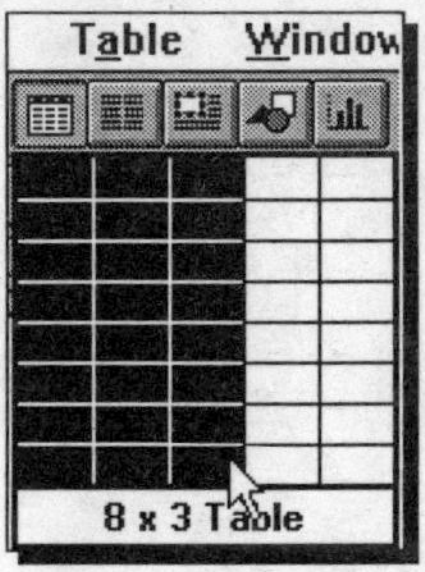

As you drag the mouse, the 'Table' button expands to create the grid of rows and columns shown here. At the bottom of the box there is an automatic display of the number of rows and columns you are selecting by this method. When you release the mouse button, a table is inserted in your document the size of the selected grid.

For our example, we require an 9 x 5 cell table. Once this appears in position, the cursor is placed in the top left cell awaiting your input. To see more clearly the cells forming the table, select the **Table, Gridlines** command which will display the dotted lines around each cell.

To move around in a table, simply click the desired cell, or use one of the keyboard commands listed below. Now type in the information below and format your table using the **Format, Paragraph** command to align the contents of the various columns as shown. The heading does not form part of the table.

Types of Removable Discs

Description	Capacity KBytes	Price /Unit Pence	Number Bought	Cotst in £
Double-sided floppies	360	40	20	
High-density floppies	1,200	60	40	
Double-sided stiffies	720	80	60	
High-density stiffies	1,440	100	80	
Removable hard discs	105,000	6500	1	
				=====
			Total	

When you finish, save your work under the filename PCUSERS6. We will use this table to show you how you can insert expressions into cells to make your table behave as a spreadsheet.

Navigating with the Keyboard :
To navigate around a table when using the keyboard, use the following keys:

Press this	*To do this*
Tab	Moves the insertion point right one cell, in the same row, and from the last cell in one row to the first cell in the next row. If the cell contains information it highlights the contents.
Shift+Tab	Moves the insertion point left one cell. If the cell contains information it highlights the contents.
↑,↓,←, and →	Moves the insertion point within cells, between cells, and between the cells in a table and the main document text.
Home	Moves the insertion point to the beginning of the current line within a cell.
Alt+Home	Moves the insertion point to the first column in the current row.
End	Moves the insertion point to the end of the current line within a cell.
Alt+End	Moves the insertion point to the last column in the current row.
Alt+PgUp	Moves the insertion point to the top cell in the column.
Alt+PgDn	Moves the insertion point to the bottom cell in the column.

Entering Expressions:
To enter an expression into a table so that you can carry out spreadsheet type calculations, use the **Insert, Field** command, then in the **Insert Field Type** box, select '= EXPRESSION'. In the **Field Code** box, following the =, type the function (or formula) you want to use. If you want a special format for the result of the calculation, select a format in the **Instructions** box, and press the **Add** button.

For example, to calculate the cost of purchased discs in Sterling (£), type the formula shown on the screen dump displayed on the next page.

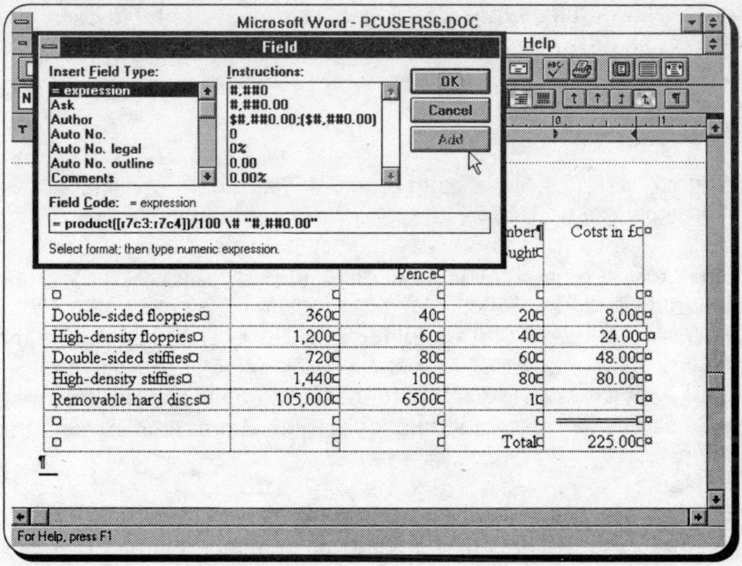

To calculate the total cost, use the following function:

=sum((r3c5:r7c5))

where "=" is the field type, "sum()" is the function, and [r3c5:r7c5] refers to the range of cells from row 3, column 5 to row 7, column 5.

In a formula you can specify any combination of mathematical and logical operators from the following list.

Addition	+
Subtraction	–
Multiplication	*
Division	/
Percent	%
Powers and roots	^
Equal to	=
Less than	<
Less than or equal to	<=
Greater than	>
Greater than or equal to	>=
Not equal to	< >

The following functions can accept references to table cells:

MIN( )
COUNT( )
MAX( )
AVERAGE( )
SUM( )
PRODUCT( )

To force a recalculation and display of a new result, use the Update Field key (F9).

The main reason for using formulas in a table, instead of just typing in the numbers, is that formulas will still give the correct final answer even if some of the data is changed. In this case you simply correct the data cells and Word recalculates the table.

Editing a Table:

You can edit a table by inserting or deleting columns or rows, merging cells, or splitting a table.

To insert a column or row - select where you want the new column or row to appear, remembering that the selected column (or row) and all columns to its right (or rows below) will move to the right (or down), then use the **Table, Insert Columns** (or **Table, Insert Rows**) command.

To delete a column or row - select the column(s) or row(s) you want to delete, then use the **Table, Delete Columns** (or **Table, Delete Rows**) command.

To merge cells - select the cells you want to merge, then use the **Table Merge Cells** command.

To split a table - move the insertion point to where you want to split the table, then use the **Table, Split** command. A blank line appears above the current row in the table, splitting it into two separate tables.

Using Table Data in a Chart:

To generate a chart from your table data, select the table with **Table, Select Table**; Word will use the data from that table to create a chart in Microsoft Graph, as described next.

Using Microsoft Graph

To chart your Word data, you must use Microsoft Graph, which is a separate program from Word. However, the program is designed to work with Word because it supports OLE (Object Linking and Embedding).

You can activate Graph by pressing the Graph button on the Toolbar, shown here. Alternatively, you can use the **Insert, Object** command and select 'Microsoft Graph' from the list in the Object dialogue box, shown below:

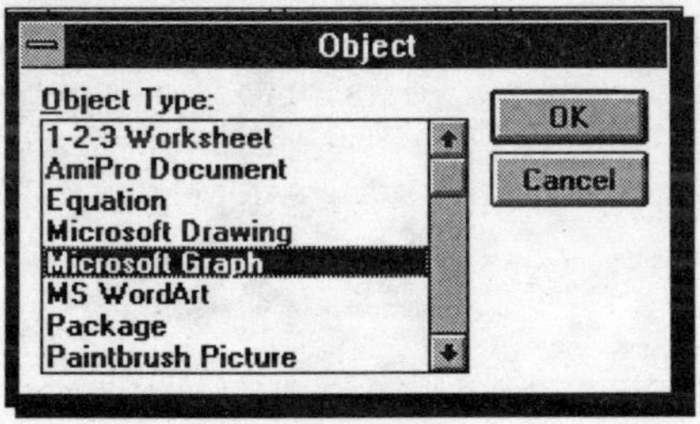

Microsoft Graph opens in an application window on top of Word, with default data in its data sheet. To change this default chart, you must change the data in the default data sheet. This can be done in various ways, but the easiest way is to either type your data directly into the displayed data sheet, or select the data from a Word table before activating Graph.

To demonstrate the way in which you can chart data held in a Word table, open the PCUSERS6 file and use your skills to copy the table entitled 'Types of Removable Discs' and place it below the original table. Then use your editing skills to transform the new table to the following:

Removable Discs	Price p/Unit	No.Bought	Cotst in £
Double-sided floppies	40	20	8.00
High-density floppies	60	40	24.00
Double-sided stiffies	80	60	48.00
High-density stiffies	100	80	80.00

Note that we have replaced 'Description' with 'Removable Discs', and that we have abbreviated the column headings so that they fit on one line. Also, we have deleted the column dealing with 'Capacity KBytes'.

Once you have made all the changes to the new table, save the file under the filename PCUSERS7. Then select the changed table, by either highlighting it, or using the **Table, Select Table** command, then activate Microsoft Graph. If you don't select a table, Graph displays its default table and chart, as follows:

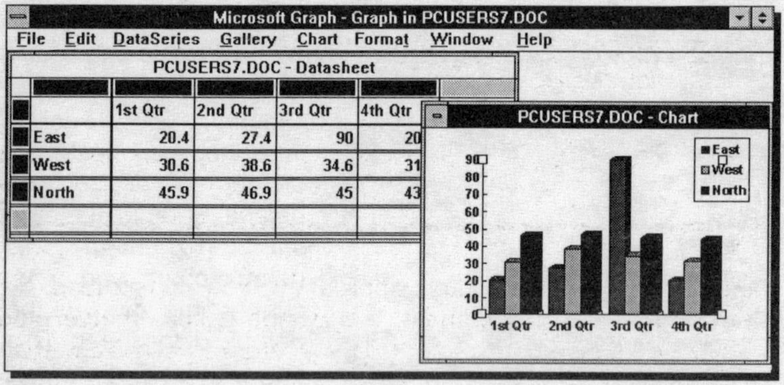

If you select a table, what should appear on your screen, after Graph displays its default table and associated chart, is:

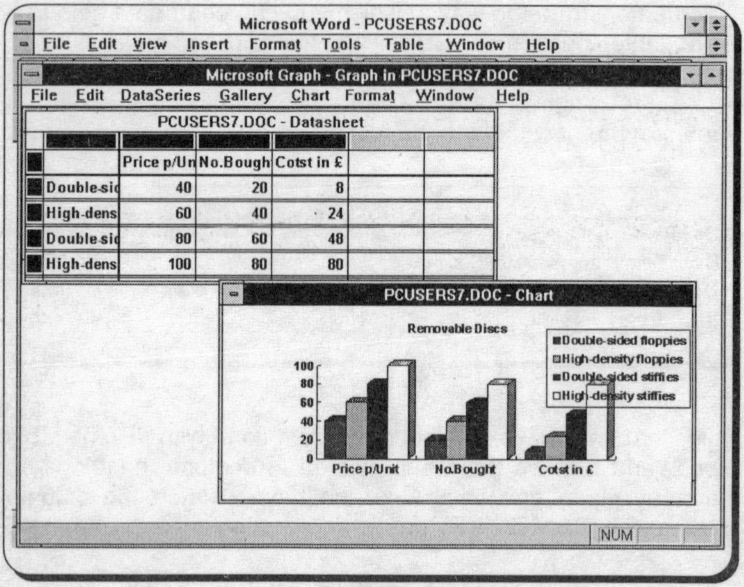

Note that the text we included in cell r1c1, was taken by Graph as the title for our chart.

You can add various items to a chart, such as titles, data labels, floating text, legends, arrows and gridlines. All these can be added with the use of the **Chart** command which displays an appropriate sub-menu with all the required options, as shown below.

When you close the Graph application, you can embed the chart in your Word document; you will be asked whether you want to update the document. If you answer with **Yes**, then Word will include your chart within a frame and place it under the table containing the data from which it was drawn. To access Microsoft Graph double-click at the frame containing your chart. Graph will be activated with the chart ready in place for further work.

Types of Chart:

Various types of charts can be selected by choosing the **Gallery** option from the Graph menu, which displays the following options:

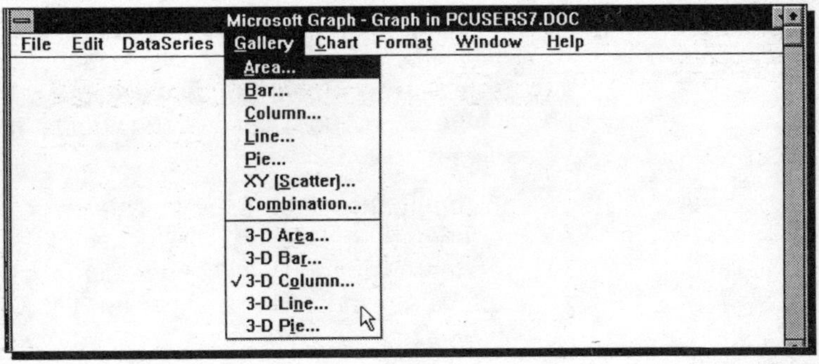

Selecting anyone of these **Gallery** options, displays a choice of up to 8 separate types of charts. For example, selecting the **3-D Area** option, displays the following:

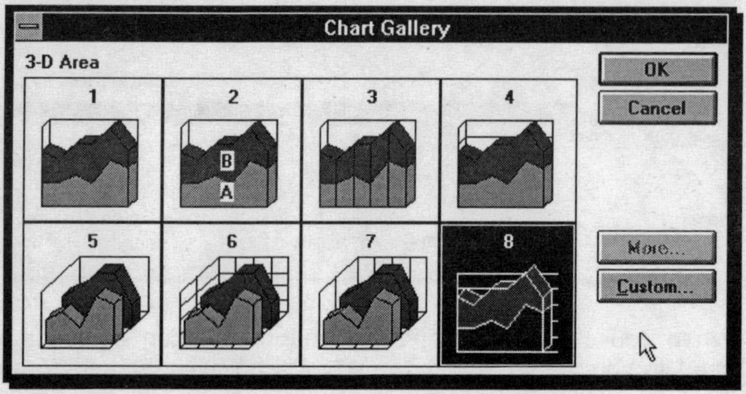

To see your chart in a different form, select your chart, then choose one of the displayed options and press **OK**. Your graph is immediately redrawn to reflect your choice of chart type. Try some of these options and watch the results.

The chart types available in the **Gallery** sub-menu (described from top to bottom), are normally used to show the following relationships between data:

Area	for comparing value changes to the total over a period of time. The 100% option shows relationships to the whole.
Bar	for comparing differences in data. Displays the values of dependent variables as two-dimensional horizontal bars. The stacked and 100% options show relationships to the whole.
Column	for comparing differences in data over a period of time. Displays the values of dependent variables as two-dimensional vertical columns. The stacked and 100% options show relationships to the whole.

Line	for representing data values with points joined by lines and appearing at equal intervals along the x-axis. For such charts, the x-axis could be intervals in time, such as labels representing months.
Pie	for comparing parts with the whole. Displays data blocks as slices of a pie. Can contain only one series.
XY (Scatter)	for showing the relationship, or degree of relationship, between numeric values in different groups of data. Used for finding patterns or trends in data (whether variables are dependent on or affect one another).
Combination	for displaying related data measured in different units (up to four axes can be used in a combination chart); used for comparing two different kinds of data or to show correlation that might be difficult to recognise.

Improving a Word Chart:

A Word chart is in fact a Microsoft Draw file. Each value in the data used to create the chart, is a separate object within the chart. You can edit the chart by selecting either the **Chart** or **Format** command. You can then use any of the sub-menu options to move or modify selected objects, including text objects, or create new objects in the chart.

In the example shown on the next page, the title of the chart was edited by selecting it and then using the **Format**, **Font** command and choosing size 12; the legend object was moved to the bottom of the chart by selecting it and using the **Format**, **Legend** command then choosing the Bottom option, and the height of the chart was increased to accommodate the new legend position without diminishing the actual size of the chart columns. Finally, an arrow was added, to emphasise a point, by using the **Chart, Add Arrow** command, then moving it appropriately. Try all these options.

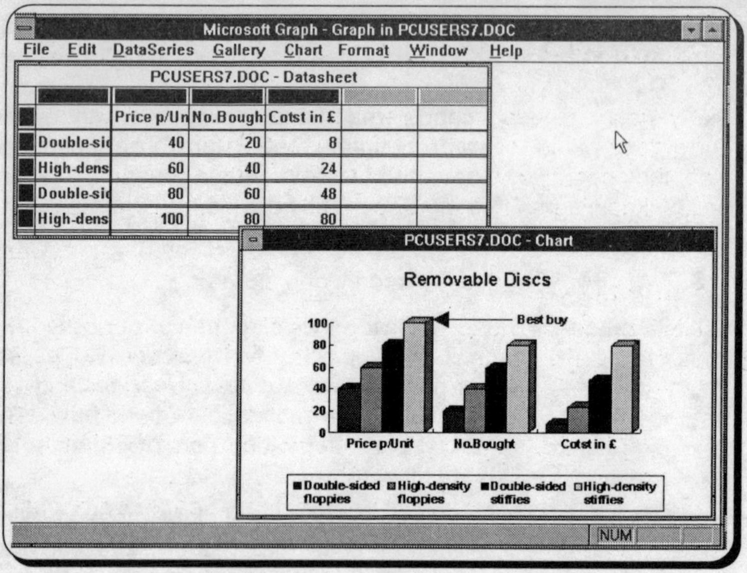

Adding Floating Text:

To add the floating text against the arrow, shown above, make sure that no other text is selected, and then just type what you want to appear on your chart. Your text appears in a box surrounded by black handles, indicating that it can be resized and moved. When you finish moving the text to its required position, press <Esc>, or click outside it.

When you have carried out all these changes to your chart within Graph, return to your document using the **File, Update** command, then save the changed Word document as PCUSERS8, using the **File, Save As** command.

We are sure that you will get many hours of fun with the various features of Microsoft Graph and, more to the point, produce some very professional graphics for your report presentations within Word.

9. MANAGING LARGE DOCUMENTS

Many users' needs might demand that they work with either large documents, or with documents which are split into many files; they might even have to automate certain routines. In such cases, knowing something about outlines, file management and design of macros is imperative.

Outline Mode

Outline mode provides a way of viewing and organising the contents of a document. Nine outline levels can be used and these could be based on formatted headings (Heading 1, Heading 2, through to Heading 9), plus Normal text. By assigning each heading level a different paragraph style, it allows easy assimilation of the contents of a document.

The following display shows part of the first page of Chapter 1 of this book in the Normal editing view.

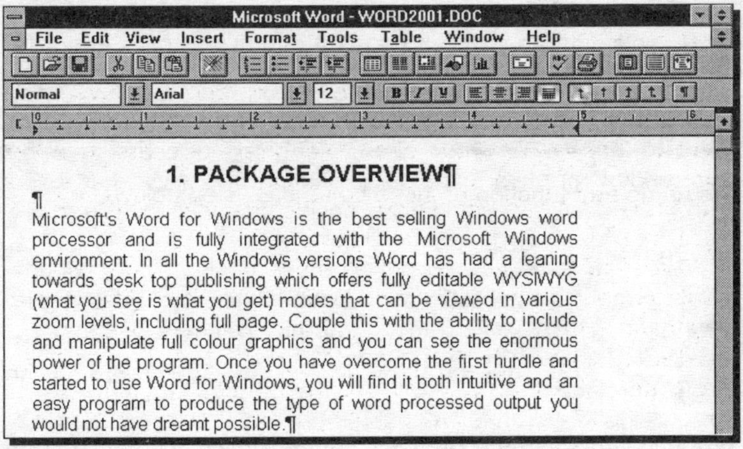

The same chapter is shown on the next page in outline view by selecting the **View, Outline** command. However, before you can see exactly what is shown here, you must assign styles to the various Headings. This can be done by selecting the outline view and assigning heading levels to your work using the tools on the outline bar which has replaced the ruler.

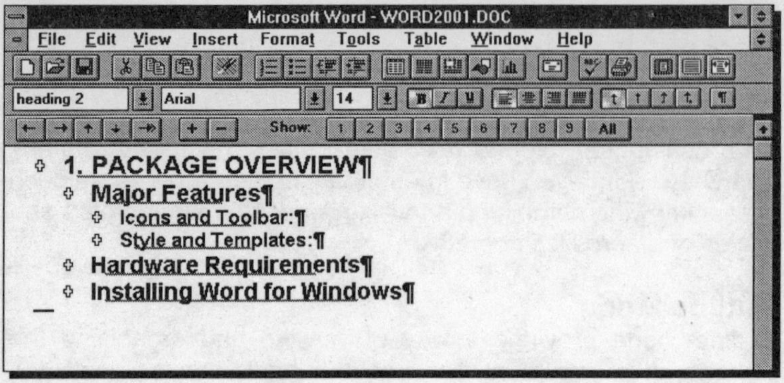

Assigning Outline Levels:

'Outline' levels are stored as part of the formatting information in the paragraph styles, so you must assign these levels to your paragraph styles before you can usefully use 'Outline' mode. Then your outline will automatically display your document headings at the correct levels. This is an easy process carried out by selecting an existing heading and clicking in the outline bar one of the following buttons:

The name and function of these buttons is listed below.

Buttons	***Name***	***Function***
	**Promote**	Assigns heading to a higher outline level.
	**Demote**	Assigns to a lower outline level.
	**Move Up**	Moves selected text before the paragraph preceding it.
	**Move Down**	Moves selected text after the paragraph following it.
	**Double Arrow**	Demotes a heading to body text.

[+]	**Plus**	Displays hidden subordinate headings until text is reached.
[−]	**Minus**	Hides displayed subordinate text or lower level headings.
[1] to [9]		Displays all headings and text to the lowest selected level.
[All]	**Display All**	Displays all text if some is collapsed, else displays headings if all text is expanded.

Using the expand and collapse commands, you can display the entire document or only selected text. Editing a document in 'Outline' mode is simple because you can control the level of detail that displays and quickly see the structure of the document. If you want to focus on the main topics in the document, you can collapse the text to display only paragraph styles set to high outline levels. If you want to view additional detail, you can expand the text to display text using paragraph styles set to lower outline levels.

Outline Buttons:
Another feature of the 'Outline' mode is the buttons placed before each paragraph. These not only show the status of the paragraph, but can be used to quickly manipulate paragraph text. Referring to the screen display on the next page, the buttons placed before each paragraph have the following meaning:

Plus button - Indicates that the paragraph is using a paragraph style set to an outline level between 1 and 9 and that the paragraph has subordinate text.

Minus button - Indicates that the paragraph is using a paragraph style set to an outline level between 1 and 9 and that the paragraph does not have any subordinate text.

Box button - Indicates that the paragraph is using a paragraph style set to an outline level of Normal text.

To display, or hide, subordinate text double-click a 'Plus' button. Click on a 'Plus' button and drag it, to move text to a new location. Word automatically moves the text as you drag the mouse.

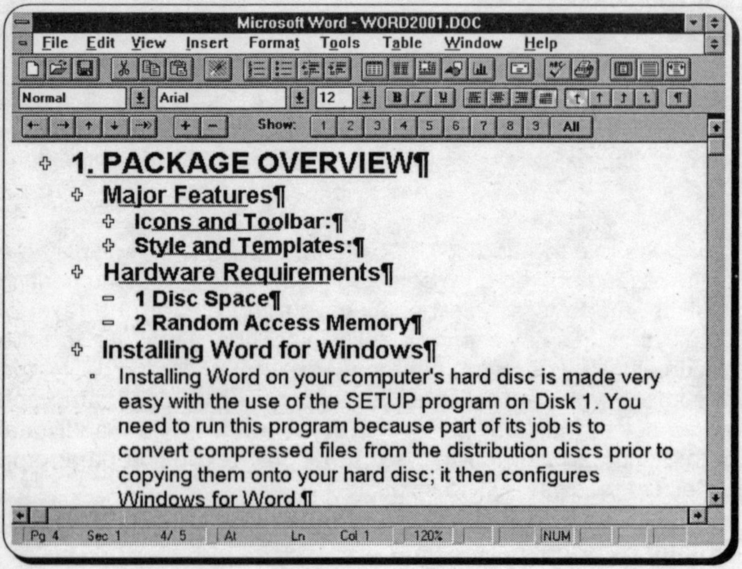

If you print from 'Outline' mode only the text that is exposed on the screen will actually print. Subordinate text and the outline buttons do not print.

Outline Numbering:
If you want all your paragraphs numbered, you must rank all the styles and then assign one of the numbering schemes in the dialogue box obtained with the use of the **Tools, Bullets and Numbering** command, as shown on the next page. As you can see, if you were in Outline mode before invoking the dialogue box, then the third button at the top of the dialogue box is selected and, therefore, your choice is for outline numbering. If you were in any other mode, you should first activate the **Outline** button to obtain the relevant dialogue box.

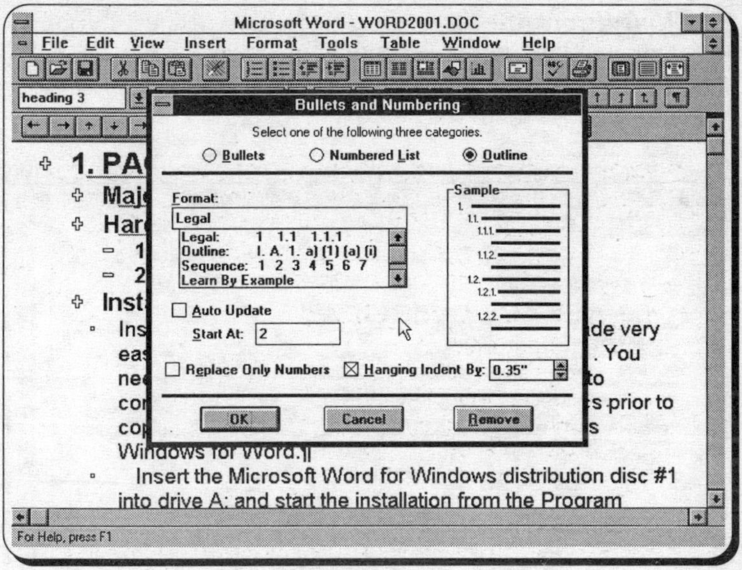

The choice between numbering schemes is: Legal, Outline, Sequence, Learn By Example, and Outline All.

Creating a Table of Contents:

To create a table of contents from outlining, position the insertion point where you want the table of contents to appear, and use the **Insert, Table of Contents** command which displays the following dialogue box:

If you are using heading paragraphs, then select this option on the dialogue box. You then select either the **All** option, or the **From: To:** option. With the latter selection, you can specify the lowest and highest heading levels you want to use. On pressing **OK** the table of contents is formed, ready for you to format to your requirements.

File Management

The first time you use the **File, Find File** command, Word searches the current directory and produces a list of available files and displays them within the following dialogue box.

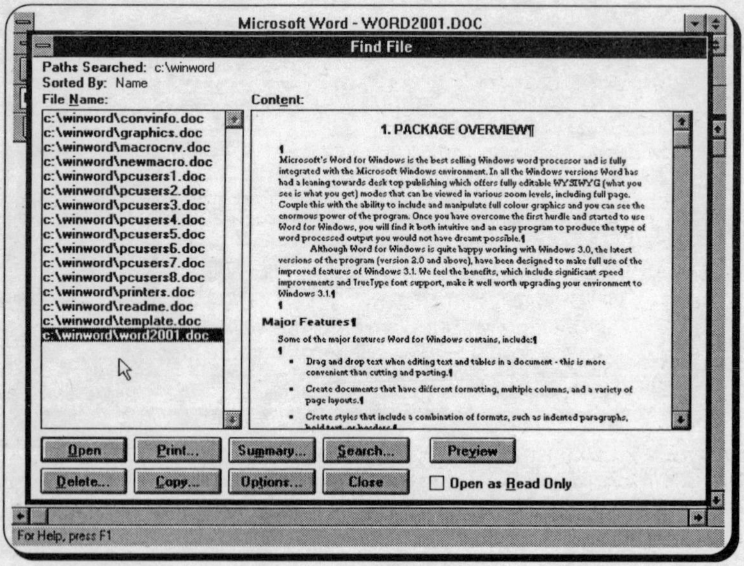

The first file is normally highlighted and its contents are displayed in the **Contents** box. As you select another file from the list, Word displays its contents too.

You can change what is shown in the above listing by pressing the **Options** button. From the displayed dialogue box, shown below, you can select one of the 'Sort Files By' options,

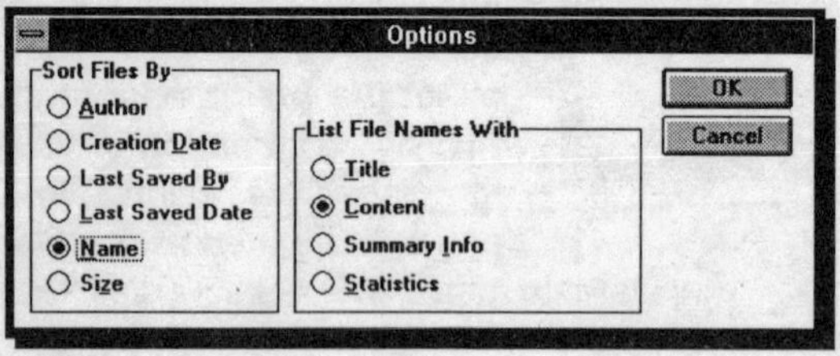

to have files listed by author, date, name of last person who saved the files, date with most recent date first, name of file (the default option), or size of file. File names can be listed with title, content, summary information, or statistics.

Once you have selected the options for the display of your files, you can select a file from the list by clicking on its name. A double-click opens the file. To select a group of files, point to the first file in the group, press the left mouse button and while pressed drag the mouse pointer downwards to highlight the required number of files, then release the mouse button. Alternatively, click at the first file in the group, hold the <Shift> key down and click at the last file in the group. All files in between are highlighted to indicate they have been selected, as shown below:

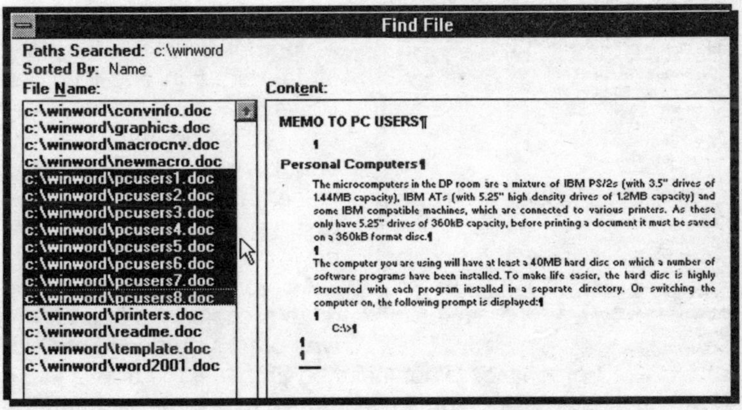

Once selected, files can be opened, printed, deleted, or copied.

If you want to search for a different type of file, and/or for files in a different directory, then use the **Search** button which displays the following dialogue box:

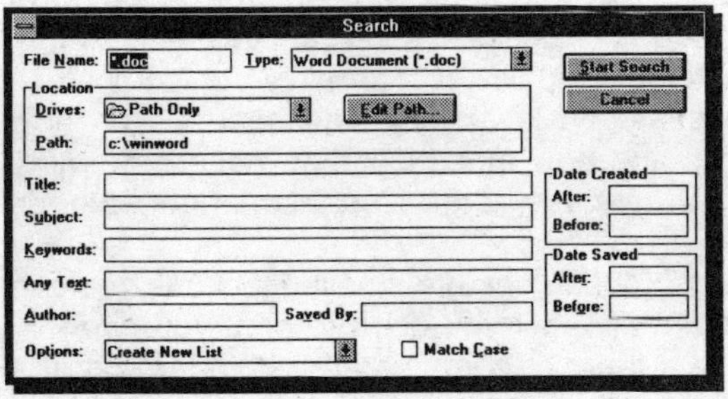

From here you can change the **File Name** and **Type** of files, the 'Location' of the files, by specifying the drive and path, then select the criteria for the search, such as title, subject, keywords, etc.

Importing and Exporting Data

To make Word an easy package for people to convert to, Microsoft have provided a list of file conversion 'filters', which enable you to import document and data files made in other packages. You can export Word files to some of these packages as well.

If you select to open a file that Word does not recognise as its own, then the following dialogue box is displayed so that you can choose one of the options offered.

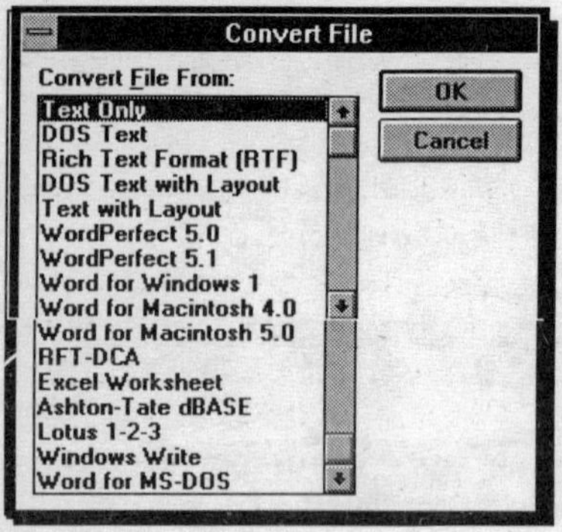

The list of available filters, shown in this dialogue box, is a composite one; it displays all the filters in one long list. However, when the dialogue box is first opened, you will only be able to see the top half of this list, and to see the rest, you must press the down arrow scroll button.

As you can see, there is quite a choice of filters. If the type of files produced by your current word processor is not included amongst the above list, it might be possible for you to export your document from the other word processor to a common file format such as; 'Rich Text Format', or 'Text with Layout'.

Assembling Long Documents

If you are involved in writing long documents, such as books, it is best if you split each document into sections (or chapters) of approximately 20 pages long. Anything above this length, particularly if it contains graphics, will strain your computer's resources. How much strain is experienced depends on how fast your computer is and how much Random Access Memory (RAM) it contains. In any case, large files take longer to open and save.

Having broken a long document into smaller sections you can work with these separately until you need to print your work in its entirety, or create a table of contents and an index with the page numbers. You will then need to create a 'Master Document', which can be achieved with the use of field codes.

One method of doing this is by using the **Insert, File** command, selecting the file you want to link, say PCUSERS3, in the displayed dialogue box, then clicking the **Link to File** box so that it appears with a check mark, as shown here, and pressing **OK**. Now, what you should see on your screen is the INCLUDE field with the filename of the file you want to link. If instead the actual document is displayed, then select the **View** command and turn on the **Field Codes** option (it is on, when a tick appears against it). After the first line of the following display appears on your screen, press <Enter> to move the insertion point to a new line.

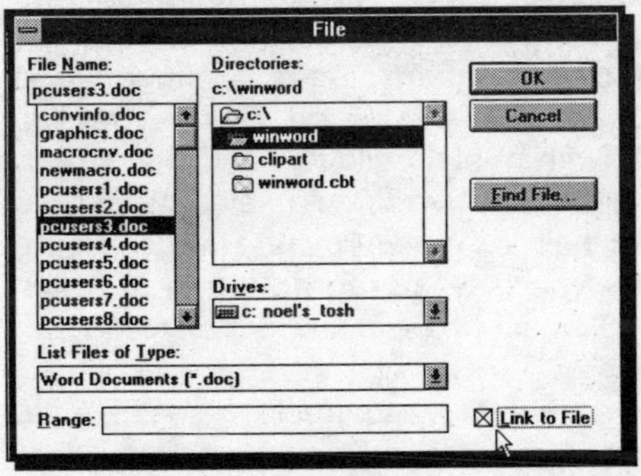

To link the other files (PCUSERS4.DOC & PCUSERS5.DOC), repeat twice the **Insert, File** command, select the filename, check the **Link to File** box and press **OK**, followed by <Enter>.

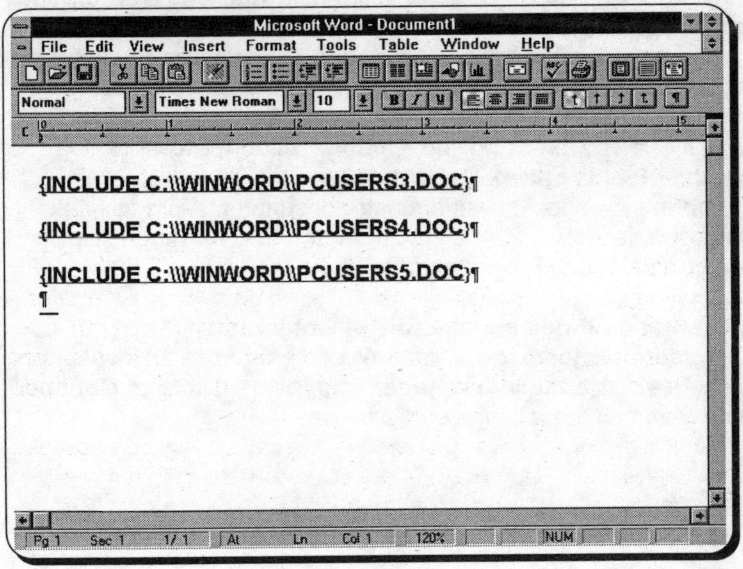

Note the way in which the path of the file appears with double backslashes within the INCLUDE field. This is important if you were to actually use the second method of linking files together, which involves the use of the **Insert, Field** command and selecting the INCLUDE field from the 'Insert Field Type' list, then typing in the full path (with \\) of the file to be linked.

There is an additional option that you could select within the 'File' dialogue box which has to do with the **Range** of the selected file. Were you to type, say, **paragraph50** in this box, all paragraphs from 1 to 50 would be included in the linking, but not the rest.

To verify that all of the above works correctly, use the **File, Print Preview** command to view what you would get if you were to print to paper. This saves your printer and a few trees!

Printing a Master Document:

When you are finally ready to print the linked files to paper, first select each file in turn, move the insertion point to the end of the selected document and use the **Insert, Break** command, and choose the **Next Page** option. This ensures that when you print the assembled document, each section of it appears on a new page.

Next, return to the master document (the one that displays the INCLUDE fields), select all the INCLUDE field lines and press the **F9** function key which has the effect of updating the links to reflect the changes made to the source documents. Updating can also be done from within the **File, Print** command, by pressing the **Options** button and selecting the **Update Fields** option.

When you elect to print a master document, Word collates the various sections of the document into one large file and numbers the pages sequentially.

Creating an Index and a Table of Contents:

To create an index or a table of contents from an assembled document, use the **Insert, Index** and **Insert, Table of Contents** commands, as explained earlier.

Word Macros Basics

A macro is simply a set of instructions made up of a sequence of keystrokes, mouse selections, or of commands stored in a macro file. After saving, or writing, a macro and attaching a quick key combination to it, you can run the same sequence of commands whenever you want. This can save a lot of time and, especially with repetitive operations, can save mistakes creeping into your work.

In Word there are two basic ways of creating macros. The first one is generated by the program itself, recording and saving a series of keystrokes, or mouse clicks. The second one involves the use of WordBASIC, the programming language that comes with Word for Windows. With this method, you can write quite complex macro programs directly into a macro file using the Word for Windows' macro editor.

Where to Store Macros:

You can choose where to store macros, whether you record them or program them, with the use the **File, Template** command which displays the following dialogue box:

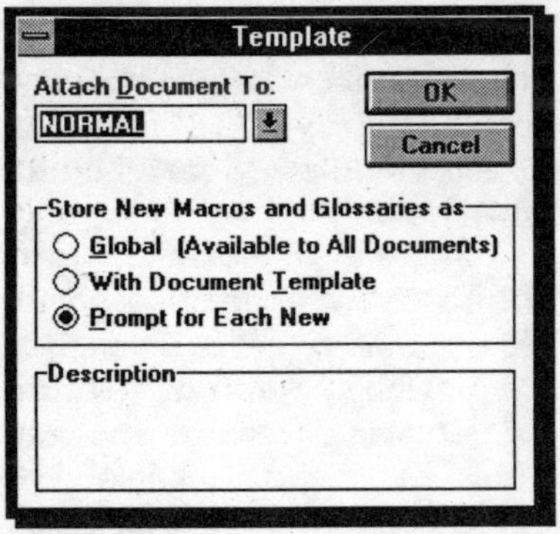

From here you can select to store macros as **Global** which stores them with your NORMAL.DOT file and makes them accessible to all documents, or **With Document Template** which makes them accessible only to documents using that particular template. It is sensible to save specialised macros with a template rather than clutter your NORMAL.DOT file with too many macros.

Macros are also stored in a third way, as 'Commands', but when you record, or program them, they can only be stored as **Global** or **With Document Template**. Macros stored as 'Commands' are built-in macros stored within the Word for Windows program, many of which appear as menu commands. These and others, that do not appear as menu commands, can be added to a toolbar button or your own macro.

To see what macro 'Commands' are available, use the **Tools, Macro** command, and select the **Commands** button which displays a list in the Macro dialogue box, shown here.

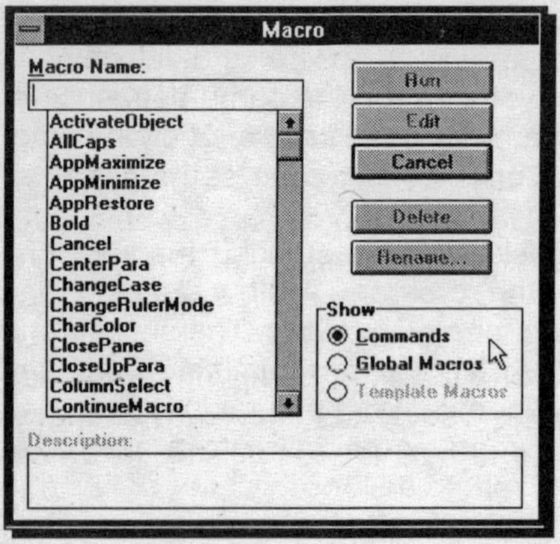

There are over 300 macro 'Commands' and as each one is selected, by highlighting it, an explanation of what it does appears in the **Description** box at the bottom of the dialogue box. It is perhaps worth spending some time examining what is available, particularly if you intend to write your own macros.

Recording a Macro:
To demonstrate how easy it is to save and name a macro, we will start with a simplistic one that enhances the word at the cursor to bold type in italics. Open PCUSERS1.DOC, place the cursor in a document word and select **Tools**, **Record Macro**, which opens the dialogue box shown below.

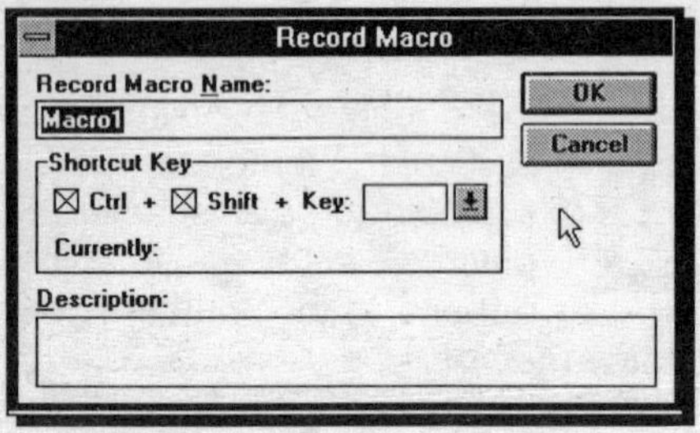

Type a name for your macro (call it Boldital) in the **Record Macro Name** window, and select a suitable key stroke combination, such as <Ctrl+Shift+I>, in the **Shortcut Key** window. Most <Ctrl> or <Shift> keys with a letter or function key combinations are suitable (press the down arrow next to the 'Key' box in the **Shortcut Key** window to obtain a list of available letters and function keys). Finally, give the macro a description, such as 'Bold & Italic', and press the **OK** button.

From this point on, all key strokes and mouse clicks (but not mouse movements in the editing area) will be recorded.

While the cursor is still placed in the word to be modified, use the key strokes, <Ctrl+→> followed by <←> followed by <Shift+Ctrl+←>, to highlight the word, then select **Bold** and **Italic**, either from the **Format**, **Character** menu, or by clicking their buttons on the Ribbon. Press <→>, to cancel the highlight and select the **Tools, Stop Recorder** command. Your macro should now be recorded and held in memory.

Saving a Macro to Disc:

To save your macro to disc, use the **File, Save All** command. Word first asks you whether you would like to save any changes made to opened documents and templates, then the following dialogue box is displayed:

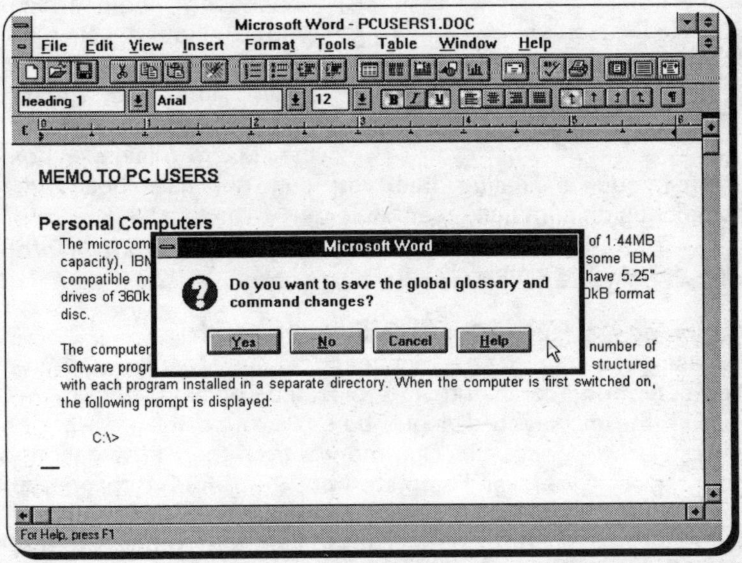

This is the prompt to save a global macro. If you were saving a template macro, then a similar prompt would appear on the screen, but with the template name specified. In either case, choose **Yes** to save the macro.

Playing Back a Macro:

There are three main ways of activating a macro. You can use the playback shortcut keys straight from the keyboard. In our case place the cursor in another word and press <Ctrl+Shift+I>. The word should be enhanced automatically. If not check back that you carried out the instructions correctly.

The second method is to select the **Tools**, **Macro** command, then select the macro from the list, as shown here, and press the **Run** button. From this dialogue box you can also **Edit**, **Delete**, or **Rename** a selected macro. The actual list that appears in the **Macro Name** box is dependent on which **Show** button is active. If the **Commands** button is active, then the **Delete** and **Rename** buttons of the Macro dialogue box are dimmed, indicating that you can not use these two commands on command macros.

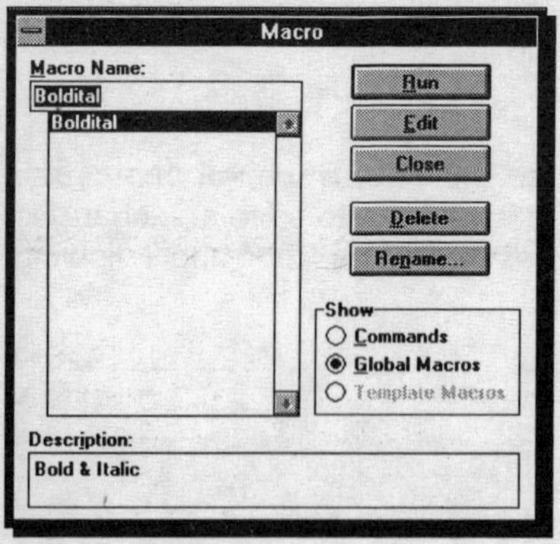

The last method is to attach the macro to a custom button on the Toolbar, and simply click it.

Attaching Macros or Commands to the Toolbar:

To assign a macro or a command to the Toolbar, use the **Tools, Options** command, and select the Toolbar **Category.**

From the displayed dialogue box, shown on the next page, choose either **Macros** or **Commands** from the **Show** options. Next, select **Global** or **Template** from the **Context** option and highlight the required command or macro from the displayed list. Finally, scroll through the **Tool to Change** list until you find the button you want to change, then scroll through the **Button** list, choose an appropriate one, and press the **Change** button. The Toolbar reflects your changes immediately, after which you can return to your editing screen, by pressing the **Close** button.

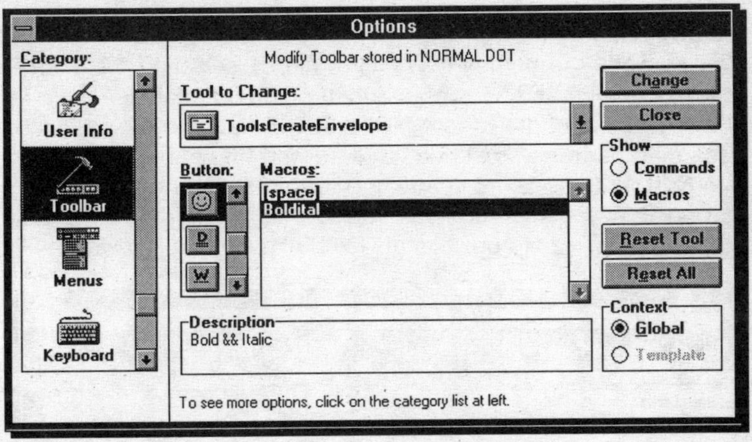

Attaching Macros or Commands to Menus:

The process of attaching macros or commands to menus is similar to attaching them to the Toolbar, as described previously. If you have gone through that procedure, you should find what follows quite simple.

To add a macro or command to the menu, use the following steps:

(a) Select the **Tools, Options** command, then select the Menus **Category**, which causes the Options dialogue box to be displayed.

(b) From the **Show** options, choose **Macros** or **Commands**, then select either **Global** or **Template** from the **Context** box.

(c) From the **Commands/Macros** list box choose a macro or command; if you want to add a separator line to the menu, choose the dashed line from the list. Next, select from the **Menu** list the menu to which you want to attach the macro or command.

(d) Type the name of the macro or command in the **Menu Text** list box with an ampersand (&) before the letter you want underlined as the activating letter.

(e) Press the **Add** button, followed by the **Close** button.

To remove a macro or command from a menu, repeat steps (a) to (c), then select from the **Menu Text** list the menu item you want to remove, and press the **Delete** button.

Editing a Macro:
You can edit the entries in a macro file by selecting the **Tools, Macros**, command which opens the Macro dialogue box in which you select the macro file to edit. Select the 'Boldital' file, assuming of course that you saved it with that name, and press the **Edit** button. Word loads the file into the normal editing screen and you treat the macro file exactly the same as any other. The listing of our Boldital file should look as follows:

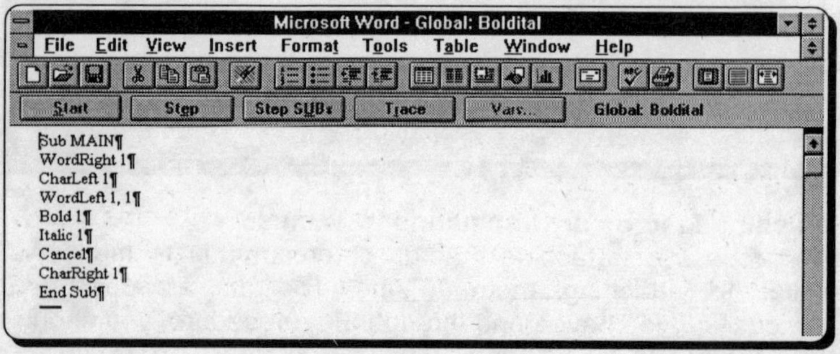

If you look at this listing you will see that it would be very easy to edit the commands in the file. If you do edit it, you should then save the file with the **File, Save All** command.

Notice the following two aspects in the screen display above:

(a) when editing a macro, the Ribbon is replaced by a macro editing bar, and

(b) Macros within WordBASIC are considered to be 'subroutines' that run under Word for Windows.

The buttons on the macro editing bar have the following functions:

Button	***Function***
Start/Continue	Starts macro execution or continues execution after a pause. When the macro is paused, the Start button changes to Continue.
Step	Executes the macro one statement at a time, highlighting the statement and pausing until the Step button is pressed again.

Step SUBs	Executes the macro one subroutine at a time, highlighting the first line of the following subroutine and pausing until the Step SUB button is pressed again.
Trace	Executes the macro from start to finish, one statement at a time and highlighting the statement being executed.
Vars	Shows the current value of the variables used in the macro and allows you to reset these during macro execution.

Word's Sample Macros

Word for Windows comes with several sample macros which are associated with templates saved in the **winword** directory, and can be copied to your own documents or templates. To find out what the sample macros can do, open the file NEWMACRO.DOC. This lists some instructions, then displays a dialogue box with a list of useful macros, as shown below.

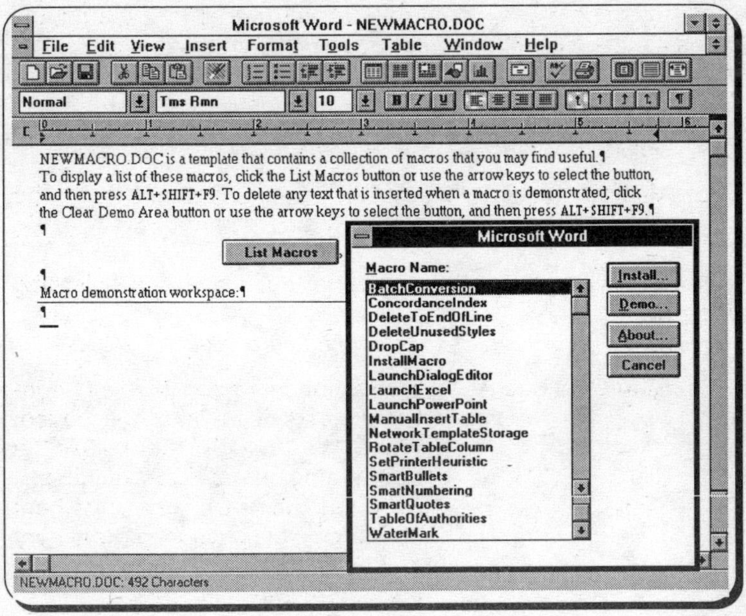

To read the instructions, simply move the dialogue box out of the way, which is exactly what we have done on the screen dump. In fact, this screen is a composite display, showing all the available macros at once. You will have to use the scroll button of the dialogue box to see the last few files.

To learn what these powerful macros can do, simply select one, by highlighting it, and press the **Demo** button. To add a macro to the global menu, click the **Install** button. We suggest you spend some time studying these macros; you will learn a lot and will no doubt find quite a few useful utilities amongst them.

Combining these sample macros with the **Tools Options** Toolbar and Menu commands, you can customise Word for Windows to suit your word processing needs.

APPENDIX A
KEYBOARD SHORTCUTS

Function Key Shortcuts:
To execute commands quickly, press the following function keys or function key combinations:

Command	***Press***
Activate annotation, header/footer outline or macro menu bar	Shift+F10
All lower case	Shift+F3
Close file	Ctrl+F4
Copy text	Shift+F2
Decrease font size	Ctrl+Shift+F2
Enlarge application window	Alt+F10
Enlarge document window	Ctrl+F10
Exit file	Alt+F4
Extend selection	F8
Field characters	Ctrl+F9
Field codes or results	Shift+F9
Find next	Shift+F4
Go To	F5
Go To/Macro button fields	Alt+Shift+F9
Help	F1
Increase font size	Ctrl+F2
Insert Bookmark	Ctrl+Shift+F5
Insert glossary or spike	F3
Insert spike and empty contents	Ctrl+Shift+F3
Lock field	Ctrl+F11
Menu bar	F10
Move text	F2
Move window	Ctrl+F7
Next field	Alt+F1
Next pane	F6
Next window	Alt+F6
Open file	Ctrl+F12
Preceding application window size	Alt+F5
Preceding document window size	Ctrl+F5
Preceding field	Alt+Shift+F1
Preceding pane	Shift+F6
Preceding position	Shift+F5

Preceding window	Alt+Shift+F6
Print file	Ctrl+Shift+F12
Reduce application to icon	Alt+F9
Repeat edit	F4
Save file	Alt+Shift+F2
Save As file	Alt+F2
Shrink selection	Shift+F8
Size window	Ctrl+F8
Spelling tool	F7
Store in spike	Ctrl+F3
Thesaurus tool	Shift+F7
Toggle tab & paragraph marks	Ctrl+Shift+F8
Unlink field	Ctrl+Shift+F9
Unlock field	Ctrl+Shift+F11
Update field	F9
Update link	Ctrl+Shift+F7
What is - help	Shift+F1

Shortcuts for Navigating and Selecting Text:

You can move the cursor around a document with the normal direction keys, and with the key combinations shown below. To select text, press the <Shift> key and hold it pressed prior to using the navigational key combinations:

To Move	***Press***
Left one character	←
Right one character	→
Up one line	↑
Down one line	↓
Left one word	Ctrl+←
Right one word	Ctrl+→
Beginning of line	Home
End of line	End
Paragraph beginning	Ctrl+↑
Paragraph end	Ctrl+↓
Up one screen	PgUp
Down one screen	PgDn
Top of previous page	Ctrl+PgUp
Top of next page	Ctrl+PgDn
To beginning of file	Ctrl+Home
To end of file	Ctrl+End

Shortcuts for Editing Text:

You can search for, and replace, tabs and hard returns, or a combination of both these and text. The list below gives the key combinations of special characters to type into the **Find** and **Replace With** boxes.

Specifying Text

To find or replace	***Type***
A caret character	^^
A question mark	^?
An optional hyphen	^–
A nonbreaking hyphen	^~
A section mark, or hard page break	^d
A newline character	^n
A paragraph mark	^p
A nonbreaking space	^s
A tab character	^t
A white space	^w
Any single character	?

Inserting Hyphens and Non-breaking Spaces

To Insert	***Press***
Non-breaking hyphen	Shift+Ctrl+<–>
Non-breaking space	Shift+Ctrl+<Spacebar>
Optional hyphen	Ctrl+<–>

Shortcuts for Formatting:

To format text or paragraphs, use the following shortcut key combinations:

Character Formatting

To Format	***Press***
Bold	Ctrl+B
Colour change	Ctrl+V
Delete strikethrough text	Ctrl+Z
Double underline	Ctrl+D
Font Name	Ctrl+F
Hidden	Ctrl+H

Italic	Ctrl+I
New text	Ctrl+N
Point size	Ctrl+P
Remove character formatting	Ctrl+Space
Small capitals	Ctrl+K
Underline	Ctrl+U
Word Underline	Ctrl+W

Paragraph Formatting

To Format	***Press***
Centred lines	Ctrl+C
Close space before	Ctrl+E
Justify lines	Ctrl+J
Left-aligned lines	Ctrl+L
Open space before	Ctrl+O
Right-aligned lines	Ctrl+R
Remove paragraph formatting	Ctrl+X
Single-spaced lines	Ctrl+1
Double-spaced lines	Ctrl+2
One-and-a-half-spaced lines	Ctrl+5

Shortcuts for Navigating in Tables:
To navigate around a table when using the keyboard, use the following keys:

To Move	***Press***
To bottom cell in column	Alt+PgDn
To end of the current line in cell	End
To first column of current row	Alt+Home
To last column in current row	Alt+End
Left one cell	Shift+Tab
Right one cell	Tab
To start of current line in cell	Home
To top cell in column	Alt+PgUp
Within cells & in between cells	↑,↓,←, and →

APPENDIX B
WORD'S AVAILABLE BUTTONS

The Default Toolbar Buttons:
The default Toolbar contains 22 buttons which have the following effect:

Button	***Effect***
	Creates a new document based on the NORMAL.DOT template.
	Opens an existing document or template.
	Saves the active document or template.
	Cuts the selection and puts it on the clipboard.
	Copies the selection and puts it on the clipboard.
	Pastes the clipboard contents at the insertion point.
	Reverses the last action.
	Creates a numbered list based on the current defaults.
	Creates a bulleted list based on the current defaults.

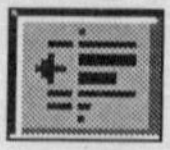

Moves the left indent to the previous tab stop.

Moves the left indent to the next tab stop.

Inserts a table.

Changes the column format within selected sections.

Inserts an empty frame, or frames the selected text.

Starts Microsoft Draw.

Starts Microsoft Graph.

Sets up an address for an envelope.

Checks the spelling in the active document.

Prints the active document using the current defaults.

Displays an entire page in page layout mode.

Scales the document to 100% in the normal view.

Scales the document so that the full width of the page can be seen.

The Ribbon Buttons:
The Ribbons contains 12 buttons which have the following effect:

Button	***Effect***
	Embolden or clear selected text.
	Italicise or clear selected text.
	Underline or clear selected text.
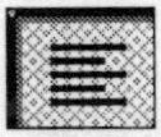	Left-align selected paragraphs.
	Centre-align selected paragraphs.
	Right-align selected paragraphs.
	Justify selected paragraphs.
	Set a left-align tab stop.
	Set a centre-align tab stop.
	Set a right-align tab stop.

Sets a decimal tab stop, aligning tab on the decimal point.

Displays and hides special non-printing characters, such as tab characters or tab marks.

INDEX

R

S

COMPANION DISC TO THIS BOOK

This book contains many pages of file/program listings. There is no reason why you should spend hours typing them into your computer, unless you wish to do so, or need the practice.

The COMPANION DISC for this book comes with all the example listings. It is available in both 3.5-inch and 5.25-inch formats.

COMPANION DISCS for all books written by the same author(s) and published by BERNARD BABANI (publishing), are also available and are listed at the front of this book. Make sure you specify the BP book number and the book title in your order.

ORDERING INSTRUCTIONS

To obtain your copy of the companion disc, fill-in the order form below, enclose a cheque (payable to **P.R.M. Oliver)** or a postal order, and send it to the address given below.

Book No.	Book Name	Unit Price	Total Price
BP ___		£3.50	
BP ___		£3.50	
BP ___		£3.50	
Name		Sub-total	£............
Address		P & P (@ 45p/disc)	£............
Disc Format 3.5-inch....... 5.25-inch.......		Total Due	£............
Send to: P.R.M. Oliver, CSM, Pool, Redruth, Cornwall, TR15 3SE			

PLEASE NOTE

The author(s) are fully responsible for providing this Companion Disc service. The publishers of this book accept no responsibility for the supply, quality, or magnetic contents of the disc, or in respect of any damage, or injury that might be suffered or caused by its use.